Learning Cython Programming
Second Edition

Learn the fundamentals of Cython to extend the legacy of your applications

Philip Herron

[PACKT] open source ✲

PUBLISHING   community experience distilled

BIRMINGHAM - MUMBAI

Learning Cython Programming
Second Edition

First published: September 2013
Second Edition: February 2016

Production reference: 1160216

Published by Packt Publishing Ltd.
Livery Place
35 Livery Street
Birmingham B3 2PB, UK.

ISBN 978-1-78355-167-5

www.packtpub.com

Credits

Author
Philip Herron

Reviewer
Namit Kewat

Commissioning Editor
Priya Singh

Acquisition Editor
Indrajit Das

Content Development Editor
Priyanka Mehta

Technical Editor
Murtaza Tinwala

Copy Editor
Yesha Gangani

Project Coordinator
Izzat Contractor

Proofreader
Safis Editing

Indexer
Tejal Daruwale Soni

Production Coordinator
Manu Joseph

Cover Work
Manu Joseph

About the Author

Philip Herron is a developer who focuses his passion toward compilers and virtual machine implementations. When he was first accepted to Google Summer of Code 2010, he used inspiration from Paul Biggar's PhD on the optimization of dynamic languages to develop a proof of the concept GCC frontend to compile Python. This project sparked his deep interest in how Python works.

After completing a consecutive year on the same project in 2011, Philip applied to Cython under the Python foundation to gain a deeper appreciation of the standard Python implementation. Through this he started leveraging the advantages of Python to control the logic in systems or even add more high-level interfaces, such as embedding Flask web servers in a REST API to a system-level piece of software, without writing any C code.

Philip currently works as a software consultant for Instil Software based in Northern Ireland. He develops mobile applications with embedded native code for video streaming. Instil has given him a lot of support in becoming a better engineer.

He has written several tutorials for the UK-based Linux Format magazine on Python and loves to share his passion for the Python programming language.

Acknowledgments

To achieve writing this book, I would like to thank many people—my partner, Kirsty Johnston, for putting up with my late nights and giving me the confidence I needed; she is the best! I would like to thank my mum and dad, who have always supported me my whole life—thanks for helping me so much. Ian Lance Taylor, my mentor, from Google Summer of Code deserves a special mention. If it wasn't for him, I wouldn't be writing anything like this right now. I would like to thank Robert Bradshaw for mentoring my Cython Auto-PXD project; even though I had a lot going on at the time, he helped me get it done and pass. Special thanks to Nicholas Marriott for helping me with the Tmux code base. I would also like to thank Gordon Hamilton and Dr. Colin Turner for the all the support they have given me. Finally, I would like to thank Tara Simpson, Chris Van Es, Niall Kelly, and Matt McComb for the mentoring they have given me at Instil.

About the Reviewer

Namit Kewat is a software engineer working in Ahmedabad, India. He has expertise in developing high performance web applications. He also specializes in performing data analysis for generating financial information (XBRL). He is a keen learner and always looks forward to applying his skills for solving complex problems. This unique approach of his is paying him dividends both internally and globally. Namit is also fond of blogging. Those interested can visit his blog at http://namitkewat.github.io/

www.PacktPub.com

eBooks, discount offers, and more

Did you know that Packt offers eBook versions of every book published, with PDF and ePub files available? You can upgrade to the eBook version at www.PacktPub.com and as a print book customer, you are entitled to a discount on the eBook copy. Get in touch with us at customercare@packtpub.com for more details.

At www.PacktPub.com, you can also read a collection of free technical articles, sign up for a range of free newsletters and receive exclusive discounts and offers on Packt books and eBooks.

https://www2.packtpub.com/books/subscription/packtlib

Do you need instant solutions to your IT questions? PacktLib is Packt's online digital book library. Here, you can search, access, and read Packt's entire library of books.

Why subscribe?

- Fully searchable across every book published by Packt
- Copy and paste, print, and bookmark content
- On demand and accessible via a web browser

Table of Contents

Preface

Cython is a tool that makes writing native extensions to Python as easy as writing them in Python. For those who are unaware, you can implement Python modules as pure the C code, which will, for all intents and purposes, look and act like any Python code. This is required when implementing modules in Python, such as the built-in zip module which use native zlib under the hood. Doing this makes sense for the standard library modules part of Python, though for most users of Python, writing native modules should be the last course of action if possible.

Writing native modules is hard and requires prerequisite knowledge of how to use the garbage collector calls correctly in order to avoid memory leaks. It also requires an understanding of how the GIL is used, which changes if you are using CPython or PyPy. It also requires knowledge of the module structures and argument passing internally to the Python runtime. Therefore, it isn't a trivial process when the need arises. Cython lets us write and work with the native code without having to know anything about the Python runtime. We can write almost pure Python code that just so happens to let us manipulate C/C++ types and classes. We can call back and forth from the native code and into the Python code.

More importantly, Cython removes the complexity and intrinsicity and lets the programmer focus on solving problems.

What this book covers

Chapter 1, Cython Won't Bite, introduces core concepts and demonstrates Cython "Hello World". It discusses the typing and type conversion.

Chapter 2, Understanding Cython, acts as a reference throughout the book. We look at custom C types and function pointers. Using this, we will successfully use Python modules directly from C code.

Chapter 3, *Extending Applications*, uses everything from the previous chapters to write native Tmux commands using Python instead of C/C++.

Chapter 4, *Debugging Cython*, uses the cygdb wrapper over gdb to debug Cython code.

Chapter 5, *Advanced Cython*, introduces how well Cython can work with C++ classes and templates. In general, it also covers caveats in Cython.

Chapter 6, *Further Reading*, briefly looks at the related projects and interesting sources of new learning.

What you need for this book

For this book, I used my MacBook and an Ubuntu virtual machine (GDB is too old on Mac OS X for debugging). You will require the following on Mac OS X:

- Xcode
- Cython
- GCC/Clang
- Make
- Python
- Python con g
- Python distutils

On Ubuntu/Debian you can install everything via the following command:

```
$ sudo apt-get install build-essential gdb cython
```

I will go over this in the introduction, but as long as you have a working C compiler and Python along with Python libraries and headers installed, you will have everything you need for Cython.

Who this book is for

This book is intended for C/C++ developers who like using Python and Python users wanting to implement native C/C++ extensions to Python. As a reader, you can expect to be shown how you can develop applications with Cython with an emphasis on extending existing systems and with help on how you can approach it.

Extending legacy systems can be difficult, but the rewards can be great. Consider low-level thread-aware or I/O-sensitive operations in C and maintain the logic handled and provided by Python. This model of development can prove to be efficient and of great return to the development time, which can be particularly expensive when it comes to C applications.

It also allows for much more rapid development of the state or logic in a system. There is no need to worry about long data conversion algorithms in C to do small things and then needing to change them all again.

Conventions

In this book, you will find a number of text styles that distinguish between different kinds of information. Here are some examples of these styles and an explanation of their meaning.

Code words in text, database table names, folder names, filenames, file extensions, pathnames, dummy URLs, user input, and Twitter handles are shown as follows: "The preferred one would be to use `pip`."

A block of code is set as follows:

```
#include <stdio.h>

int AddFunction(int a, int b) {
    printf("look we are within your c code!\n");
    return a + b;
}
```

When we wish to draw your attention to a particular part of a code block, the relevant lines or items are set in bold:

```
>>> pyximport.install()
(None, <pyximport.pyximport.PyxImporter object at 0x102fba4d0>)
>>> import helloworld
Hello World from cython!
```

New terms and **important words** are shown in bold. Words that you see on the screen, for example, in menus or dialog boxes, appear in the text like this: "Clicking the **Next** button moves you to the next screen."

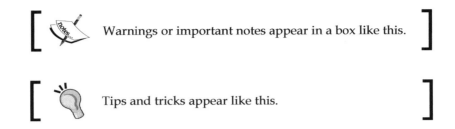

Warnings or important notes appear in a box like this.

Tips and tricks appear like this.

Reader feedback

Feedback from our readers is always welcome. Let us know what you think about this book—what you liked or disliked. Reader feedback is important for us as it helps us develop titles that you will really get the most out of.

To send us general feedback, simply e-mail feedback@packtpub.com, and mention the book's title in the subject of your message.

If there is a topic that you have expertise in and you are interested in either writing or contributing to a book, see our author guide at www.packtpub.com/authors.

Customer support

Now that you are the proud owner of a Packt book, we have a number of things to help you to get the most from your purchase.

Downloading the example code

You can download the example code files from your account at http://www.packtpub.com for all the Packt Publishing books you have purchased. If you purchased this book elsewhere, you can visit http://www.packtpub.com/support and register to have the files e-mailed directly to you.

You can download the code files by following these steps:

1. Log in or register to our website using your e-mail address and password.
2. Hover the mouse pointer on the SUPPORT tab at the top.
3. Click on Code Downloads & Errata.
4. Enter the name of the book in the Search box.
5. Select the book for which you're looking to download the code files.

6. Choose from the drop-down menu where you purchased this book from.
7. Click on Code Download.

Once the file is downloaded, please make sure that you unzip or extract the folder using the latest version of:

- WinRAR / 7-Zip for Windows
- Zipeg / iZip / UnRarX for Mac
- 7-Zip / PeaZip for Linux

Errata

Although we have taken every care to ensure the accuracy of our content, mistakes do happen. If you find a mistake in one of our books—maybe a mistake in the text or the code—we would be grateful if you could report this to us. By doing so, you can save other readers from frustration and help us improve subsequent versions of this book. If you find any errata, please report them by visiting http://www.packtpub. com/submit-errata, selecting your book, clicking on the **Errata Submission Form** link, and entering the details of your errata. Once your errata are verified, your submission will be accepted and the errata will be uploaded to our website or added to any list of existing errata under the Errata section of that title.

To view the previously submitted errata, go to https://www.packtpub.com/books/ content/support and enter the name of the book in the search field. The required information will appear under the **Errata** section.

Piracy

Piracy of copyrighted material on the Internet is an ongoing problem across all media. At Packt, we take the protection of our copyright and licenses very seriously. If you come across any illegal copies of our works in any form on the Internet, please provide us with the location address or website name immediately so that we can pursue a remedy.

Please contact us at copyright@packtpub.com with a link to the suspected pirated material.

We appreciate your help in protecting our authors and our ability to bring you valuable content.

Questions

If you have a problem with any aspect of this book, you can contact us at questions@packtpub.com, and we will do our best to address the problem.

1
Cython Won't Bite

Cython is much more than a programming language. Its origin can be traced to SAGE, the mathematics software package, where it is used to increase the performance of mathematical computations such as those involving matrices. More generally, I tend to consider Cython as an alternative to SWIG to generate really good Python bindings to native code.

Language bindings have been around for years, and SWIG was one of the first and best tools to generate bindings for multitudes of languages. Cython generates bindings for Python code only, and this single purpose approach means it generates the best Python bindings you can get outside of doing it all manually, which should be attempted only if you're a Python core developer.

For me, taking control of legacy software by generating language bindings is a great way to reuse any software package. Consider a legacy application written in C/C++. Adding advanced modern features such as a web server for a dashboard or message bus is not a trivial thing to do. More importantly, Python comes with thousands of packages that have been developed, tested, and used by people for a long time that can do exactly that. Wouldn't it be great to take advantage of all of this code? With Cython, we can do exactly this, and I will demonstrate approaches with plenty of example codes along the way.

This first chapter will be dedicated to the core concepts on using Cython, including compilation, and should provide a solid reference and introduction for all the Cython core concepts.

In this first chapter, we will cover:

- Installing Cython
- Getting started - Hello World
- Using distutils with Cython

- Calling C functions from Python
- Type conversion

Installing Cython

Since Cython is a programming language, we must install its respective compiler, which just so happens to be the aptly named *Cython*.

There are many different ways to install Cython. The preferred one would be to use `pip`:

```
$ pip install Cython
```

This should work on both Linux and Mac. Alternatively, you can use your Linux distribution's package manager to install Cython:

```
$ yum install cython     # will work on Fedora and Centos
$ apt-get install cython # will work on Debian based systems.
```

For Windows, although there are a plethora of options available, following this wiki is the safest option to stay up-to-date: `http://wiki.cython.org/InstallingOnWindows`.

Emacs mode

There is an **emacs** mode available for Cython. Although the syntax is nearly the same as Python, there are differences that conflict in simply using Python-mode. You can grab `cython-mode.el` from the Cython source code (inside the `Tools` directory.) The preferred way of installing packages to emacs would be to use a package repository like `MELPA`:

To add the package repository to emacs, open your `~/.emacs` configuration file and add:

```
(when (>= emacs-major-version 24)
  (require 'package)
  (add-to-list
   'package-archives
   '("melpa" . "http://melpa.org/packages/")
   t)
  (package-initialize))
```

Once you add this and reload your configuration to install the Cython mode, you can simply run:

```
'M-x package-install RET cython-mode'
```

Once this is installed, you can activate the mode by adding this into your emacs config file:

```
(require 'cython-mode)
```

You can activate the mode manually at any time with:

```
'M-x cython-mode RET'
```

Getting the code examples

Throughout this book, I intend to show real examples that are easy to digest in order to help you get a feel of the different things you can achieve with Cython. To access and download the code used, please clone this repository:

```
$ git clone git://github.com/redbrain/cython-book.git
```

Getting started – Hello World

As you will see when running the **Hello World** program, Cython generates native Python modules. Therefore, running any Cython code, you will reference it via a module import in Python. Let's build the module:

```
$ cd cython-book/chapter1/helloworld
$ make
```

You should now have created `helloworld.so`! This is a Cython module of the same name as the Cython source code file. While in the same directory of the shared object module, you can invoke this code by running a respective Python import:

```
$ python
Python 2.7.3 (default, Aug  1 2012, 05:16:07)
[GCC 4.6.3] on linux2
Type "help", "copyright", "credits" or "license" for more information.
>>> import helloworld
Hello World from cython!
```

As you can see by opening `helloworld.pyx`, it looks just like a normal Python Hello World application, but as previously stated, Cython generates modules. These modules need a name so that they can be correctly imported by the Python runtime. The Cython compiler simply uses the name of the source code file. It then requires us to compile this to the same shared object name.

Overall, Cython source code files have the `.pyx`, `.pxd`, and `.pxi` extensions. For now, all we care about are the `.pyx` files; the others are for **cimports** and **includes** respectively within a `.pyx` module file.

The following screenshot depicts the compilation flow required to have a callable native Python module:

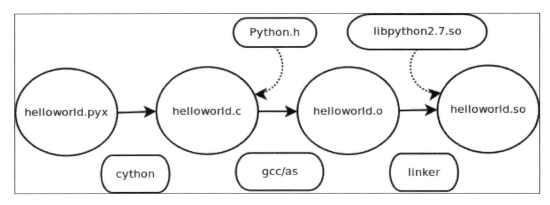

I wrote a basic `makefile` so that you can simply run `make` to compile these examples. Here's the code to do this manually:

```
$ cython helloworld.pyx
$ gcc/clang -g -O2 -fpic `python-config --cflags` -c helloworld.c -o
helloworld.o
$ gcc/clang -shared -o helloworld.so helloworld.o `python-config -
libs`
```

Using distutils with Cython

You can also compile this HelloWorld example module using Python `distutils` and `cythonize`. Open the `setup.py` along side the Makefile and you can see the alternate way to compile Cython modules:

```
from distutils.core import setup
from Cython.Build import cythonize

setup(
    ext_modules = cythonize("helloworld.pyx")
)
```

Using the `cythonize` function as part of the `ext_modules` section will build any specified Cython source into an installable Python module. This will compile `helloworld.pyx` into the same shared library. This provides the Python practice to distribute native modules as part of `distutils`.

Calling C functions from Python

We should be careful for clarity when talking about Python and Cython since the syntax is so similar. Let's wrap a simple `AddFunction` in C and make it callable from Python.

First, open a file called `AddFunction.c`, and write a simple function in it:

```
#include <stdio.h>

int AddFunction(int a, int b) {
    printf("look we are within your c code!\n");
    return a + b;
}
```

This is the C code that we will call—just a simple function to add two integers. Now, let's get Python to call it. Open a file called `AddFunction.h`, wherein we will declare our prototype:

```
#ifndef __ADDFUNCTION_H__
#define __ADDFUNCTION_H__

extern int AddFunction (int, int);

#endif //__ADDFUNCTION_H__
```

We need this so that Cython can see the prototype for the function we want to call. In practice, you will already have your headers in your own project with your prototypes and declarations already available.

Open a file called `AddFunction.pyx`, and insert the following code in it:

```
cdef extern from "AddFunction.h":
    cdef int AddFunction(int, int)
```

Here, we have to declare which code we want to call. The `cdef` is a keyword signifying that this is from the C code that will be linked in. Now, we need a Python entry point:

```
def Add(a, b):
    return AddFunction(a, b)
```

This `Add` function is a Python callable inside a `PyAddFunction` module this acts as a wrapper for Python code to be able to call directly into the C code. Again, I have provided a handy `makefile` to produce the module:

```
$ cd cython-book/chapter1/ownmodule
$ make
cython -2 PyAddFunction.pyx
gcc -g -O2 -fpic -c PyAddFunction.c -o PyAddFunction.o `python-config
--includes`
gcc -g -O2 -fpic -c AddFunction.c -o AddFunction.o
gcc -g -O2 -shared -o PyAddFunction.so AddFunction.o PyAddFunction.o
`python-config --libs`
```

Notice that `AddFunction.c` is compiled into the same `PyAddFunction.so` shared object. Now, let's call this `AddFunction` and check to see if C can add numbers correctly:

```
$ python
>>> from PyAddFunction import Add
>>> Add(1,2)
look we are within your c code!!
3
```

Notice that the print statement inside the `AddFunction` and the final result are printed correctly. Therefore, we know that the control hit the C code and did the calculation in C, and not inside the Python runtime. This is a revelation of what is possible. Python can be cited to be slow in some circumstances. Using this technique makes it possible for Python code to bypass its own runtime and to run in an unsafe context, which is unrestricted by the Python runtime which is much faster.

Type conversion in Cython

Notice that we had to declare a prototype inside the Cython source code
`PyAddFunction.pyx`:

```
cdef extern from "AddFunction.h":
    cdef int AddFunction(int, int)
```

It lets the compiler know that there is a function called `AddFunction` and it takes two
ints and returns an int. This is all the information the compiler needs to know beside
the host and target operating system's calling convention to call this function safely.
Then, we created the Python entry point, which is a Python callable that takes two
parameters:

```
def Add(a, b):
    return AddFunction(a, b)
```

Inside this entry point, it simply returned the native `AddFunction` and passed the
two Python objects as parameters. This is what makes Cython so powerful. Here,
the Cython compiler must inspect the function call and generate code to safely try
and convert these Python objects to native C integers. This becomes difficult when
precision is taken into account as well as potential overflow, which just so happens
to be a major use case since it handles everything so well. Also, remember that this
function returns an integer, and Cython also generates code to convert the integer
return into a valid Python object.

> **Downloading the example code**
>
> You can download the example code files for all Packt books you have
> purchased from your account at http://www.PacktPub.com. If you
> purchased this book elsewhere, you can visit http://www.PacktPub.
> com/support and register to have the files e-mailed directly to you.

Summary

Overall, we installed the Cython compiler, ran the Hello World example, and
took into consideration that we need to compile all code into native shared objects.
We also saw how to wrap native C code to make it callable from Python. We have
also seen the implicit type conversion which Cython does for us to make calling
C work. In the next chapter, we will delve deeper into Cython programming with
discussion on how to make Python code callable from C and manipulate native C
data structures from Cython.

2
Understanding Cython

As I mentioned previously, there are a number of methods of using Cython. As the basics are very familiar to any Python programmer, it's important to review the linking models before getting into the programming language. This is what drives the design of applications when using Cython.

Next, we will get more familiar with the Cython programming language constructs, namely, the distinction between `cdef` and `cpdef`. Then, we will look at getting the most out of Cython by interfacing directly with native C types. Later in this book, we will see that it's possible to use native C++ STL container types. This is where you will gain the optimizations in execution, as no Python runtime is required to work with native types.

Finally, we will see how easy it is to work with callbacks to and from C and Python code. This is an interesting technique whereby you can offload logic from C code to Python.

Therefore, in this chapter, we will be diving into the following topics:

*   Linking models
*   Cython keyword – cdef
*   Typedef and function pointers
*   The public keyword
*   Keyword cpdef
*   Logging from C/C++ into Python
*   Using Python ConfigParser from C/C++
*   Callbacks from Python to C/C++
*   Cython PXD
*   Integration with build systems

Linking models

Linking models are extremely important when considering how we can extend or embed things in native applications. There are two main linking models for Cython:

Fully embedded Python within C/C++ code, which looks like the following screenshot:

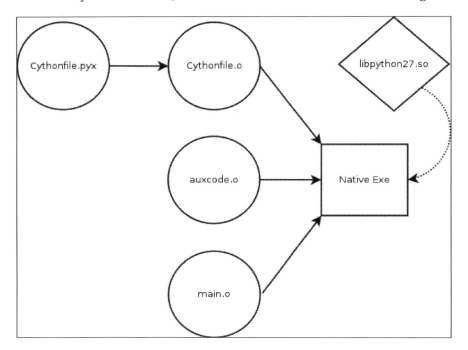

Using this method of embedding the Python runtime into a native application means you initiate execution of code directly from any point in your C/C++ code, as opposed to the *Chapter 1, Cython Won't Bite* where we had to run the Python interpreter and call an import to execute native code.

For the sake of completeness, here is the import model of using Cython:

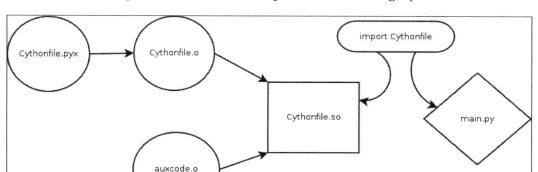

This would be a more Pythonic approach to Cython, and will be helpful if your code base is mostly Python. We will review an example of the Python `lxml` module, which provides a Cython backend, later in this book, and we can compare it to the native Python backend to review the speed and execution of both code bases to perform the same task.

Cython keyword – cdef

The `cdef` keyword tells the compiler that this statement is a native C type or native function. Remember from *Chapter 1, Cython Won't Bite* that we used this line to declare the C prototype function:

```
cdef int AddFunction(int, int)
```

This is the line that let us wrap the native C function into a Python callable using the Python `def` keyword. We can use this in many contexts, for example, we can declare normal variables for use within a function to speed up execution:

```
def square(int x):
    return x ** 2
```

This is a trivial example, but it will tell the compiler that we will always be squaring an integer. However, for normal Python code, it's a little more complicated as Python has to worry a lot more about losing precision when it comes to handling many different types. But in this case, we know exactly what the type is and how it can be handled.

You might also have noticed that this is a simple `def` function, but because it will be fed to the Cython compiler, this will work just fine, and handle the typed parameter as you would expect.

Structs

C structs can be worked with directly in Cython. For example, this header declares a simple `struct`:

```
#ifndef __MYCODE_H__
#define __MYCODE_H__

struct mystruct {
  char * string;
  int integer;
  char ** string_array;
};

extern void printStruct (struct mystruct *);

#endif //__MYCODE_H__
```

This random `struct` will demonstrate several concepts, including working with an array. Firstly, we must declare the layout of the `struct` inside Cython. We can again use the `cdef` block syntax. Everything within that block is a `cdef` and will include the specified header, which is important when the output from the Cython compiler is compiled via GCC or Clang:

```
cdef extern from "mycode.h":
  struct mystruct:
    char * string
    int integer
    char ** string_array
  void printStruct (mystruct *)
```

Now that we have declared the prototype `printStruct` function, we can use this to verify the data outside of Cython's scope. To work with this raw data type, we will make a `testStruct` Python callable, which we will invoke using a simple Python import:

```
def testStruct ():
    cdef mystruct s
    cdef char *array [2]
    s.string = "Hello World"
    s.integer = 2
    array [0] = "foo"
    array [1] = "bar"
    s.string_array = array
    printStruct (&s)
```

Let's look at this more closely. We firstly declare an instance of the `struct` on the stack. Next, we declare a C-String array of size 2. The next lines will look familiar via setting each of the members of the `struct` with a value. But notice that we declared our string array on the stack and then set the string array member to this instance. This is important as Cython will rely on the programmer to understand memory and stack versus heap properly. But it's important to notice that passing strings from language to language is completely trivial.

The final caveat with structs is while defining a `cdef` declaration for a function. If a parameter is a struct, you never declare it as follows:

```
void myfunc (struct mystruct * x)
```

Instead, we simply use the following:

```
void myfunc (mystruct * x)
```

Cython will figure it out.

There are a few subtleties with the `testStruct` function. In Cython, we have the reference operator '`&`' that works just as in C. Therefore, with this `struct` on the stack, we can pass a pointer via the reference operator just like in C.

Note that we don't have a '`→`' operator in Cython. When accessing members inside the `struct` (even if it is a pointer), we simply use the '`.`' operator. Cython understands the context and will handle it.

From the previous example and for the sake of completeness we can implement the `printStruct` function simply as:

```
#include <stdio.h>
#include "mycode.h"

void printStruct (struct mystruct * s)
{
    printf(".string = %s\n", s->string);
    printf(".integer = %i\n", s->integer);
    printf(".string_array = \n");

    int i;
    for (i = 0; i < s->integer; ++i)
        printf ("\t[%i] = %s\n", i, s->string_array [i]);
}
```

This demonstrates even when we initialize the C struct from within Cython code it's a perfectly valid C type. A simple run of this in the downloaded code is as follows:

```
$ cd chapter2/cpy-cdef-reference
$ make
$ python
>>> from mycodepy import testStruct
>>> testStruct ()
.string = Hello World
.integer = 2
.string_array =
  [0] = foo
  [1] = bar
```

This demonstrates that Cython can work with C structs—it initialized the C struct and assigned its data members, as you would expect if it was from C.

Enums

Interfacing with C enums is simple. If you have the following enum in C:

```
enum cardsuit {
    CLUBS,
    DIAMONDS,
    HEARTS,
    SPADES
};
```

Then this can be expressed as the following Cython declaration:

```
cdef enum cardsuit:
    CLUBS, DIAMONDS, HEARTS, SPADES
```

Then, use the following as the `cdef` declaration within our code:

```
cdef cardsuit card = CLUBS
```

It's a very small example, but it's important to see how simple it is.

Typedef and function pointers

The typedef in C/C++ code allows the programmer to give a new name or alias to any type. For example, one could typedef an int to myint. Or you can just simply typedef a struct so that you don't have to refer to the struct with the keyword struct every time. For example, consider this C struct and typedef:

```
struct foobar {
  int x;
  char * y;
};
typedef struct foobar foobar_t;
```

In Cython, this can be described by the following:

```
cdef struct foobar:
    int x
    char * y
ctypedef foobar foobar_t
```

Note we can also typedef pointer types as below:

```
ctypedef int * int_ptr
```

We can also typedef function C/C++ pointers, as follows:

```
typedef void (*cfptr) (int)
```

In Cython, this will be as follows:

```
ctypedef void (*cfptr)(int)
```

Using the function pointer is just as you would expect:

```
cdef cfptr myfunctionptr = &myfunc
```

There is some magic going on here with function pointers as it's simply not safe for raw Python code to directly call a Python function or vice versa. Cython understands this case and will wrap things up for us to make the call safely.

The public keyword

This is a very powerful keyword in Cython. It allows any `cdef` declaration with the `public` modifier to output a respective C/C++ header with the relative declaration accessible from C/C++. For example, we can declare:

```
cdef public struct CythonStruct:
    size_t number_of_elements;
    char ** elements;
```

Once the compiler handles this, you will have an output of `cython_input.h`:

```
struct CythonStruct {
    size_t number_of_elements;
    char ** elements;
};
```

The main caveat, if you're going to call the Python `public` declarations directly from C, is that, if your link model is fully embedded and linked against `libpython.so`, you need to use some boilerplate code to initialize Python correctly:

```
#include <Python.h>

int main(int argc, char **argv) {
    Py_Initialize ();
    // code in here
    Py_Finalize ();
    return 0;
}
```

And before calling anything with the function, you need to initialize the Python module example if you have a `cythonfile.pyx` file, and compile it with the `public` declarations as follows:

```
cdef public void cythonFunction ():
    print "inside cython function!!!"
```

You will get not only a `cythonfile.c` file, but also `cythonfile.h`, which declares a function called `extern void initcythonfile (void)`. So, before calling anything related to the Cython code, use the following:

```
/* Boiler plate init Python */
  Py_SetProgramName (argv [0]);
  Py_Initialize ();
  /* Init our config module into Python memory */
  initpublicTest ();
```

```
cythonFunction ();

/* cleanup python before exit ... */
Py_Finalize ();
```

Calling `initcythonfile` can be considered as the following in Python:

```
import cythonfile
```

Just like the previous examples, this only affects you if you're generating a fully embedded Python binary. If you are simply compiling a native module, you will not need to do this step.

Keyword cpdef

So far, we have seen two different function declarations in Cython, `def` and `cdef`, to define functions. There is one more declaration—`cpdef`. The `def` is a Python-only function, so it is only callable from Python or Cython code blocks; calling from C does not work. The `cdef` is the opposite; this means that it's callable from C and not from Python. For example, if we create a function such as:

```
cpdef public test (int x):
    ...
    return 1
```

It will generate the following function prototype:

```
__PYX_EXTERN_C DL_IMPORT(PyObject) *test(int, int __pyx_skip_
dispatch);
```

The `public` keyword will make sure we generate the needed header so that we can call it from C. Calling from pure Python, we can work with this as if it was just any other Python function. The drawback of using `cpdef` is that the native return type is `PyObject *`, which requires you to know exactly what the return type is and consult the Python API documentation to access the data. I prefer keeping bindings between the languages simpler, as this is okay for void functions, and will be easier. But if you want to return the data, it can be frustrating. For example, from the preceding code snippet, if we know that we are returning an `int` type, we could use the following:

```
long returnValue = PyInt_AsLong (test (1, 0))
```

Notice the extra argument `__pyx_skip_dispatch`. As this is an implementation-specific argument, set this to `0`, and your call should work the way you expect, taking the first parameter as the argument specified. The reason we use `long` is that every integer in Python is represented as long. You will need to refer to `https://docs.python.org/2/c-api/` for any other datatypes to get the data out of `PyObject`.

---

[17]

Note that using a public `cpdef` Cython function isn't really a good idea. Yes, it means you create functions that are callable from both C/C++ and Python with no change. But you lose the type safety which Cython can provide and is so important.

Logging from C/C++ into Python

An example of everything brought together is reusing the Python logging module directly from C. We want a few macros, such as `info`, `error`, and `debug` that can all handle a variable number of arguments and works as if we are calling a simple `printf` method.

To achieve this, we must make a Python logging backend for our C/C++ code. We need an initialization function to tell Python about our output `logfile`, and some wrappers for each `info`, `error`, and `debug`. We can simply write the public `cdef` wrappers as:

```
import logging

cdef public void initLoggingWithLogFile(const char * logfile):
    logging.basicConfig(filename = logfile,
                        level = logging.DEBUG,
                        format = '%(levelname)s %(asctime)s:
%(message)s',
                        datefmt = '%m/%d/%Y %I:%M:%S')

cdef public void python_info(char * message):
    logging.info(message)

cdef public void python_debug(char * message):
    logging.debug(message)

cdef public void python_error(char * message):
    logging.error(message)
```

Remember that we declare our public functions as `cdef`; if they were simply `def`, they wouldn't be callable from C/C++. We can make this even more awesome by using C99 `__VA_ARGS__` (this allows us to pass a variable number of arguments to a function hence the name variable arguments, this is how `printf` works) and a compiler attribute that enforces argument checking like the warnings and errors you get from wrong format specifiers when using the `printf` family of functions. Now, we can declare and define our C API to use the Python logging backend:

```
#ifndef __NATIVE_LOGGING_H__
#define __NATIVE_LOGGING_H__
```

```
#define printflike __attribute__ ((format (printf, 3, 4)))

extern void printflike native_logging_info(const char *, unsigned,
const char *, ...);
extern void printflike native_logging_debug(const char *, unsigned,
const char *, ...);
extern void printflike native_logging_error(const char *, unsigned,
const char *, ...);

#define info(...)  native_logging_info(__FILE__, __LINE__, __VA_
ARGS__)
#define error(...) native_logging_debug(__FILE__, __LINE__, __VA_
ARGS__)
#define debug(...) native_logging_error(__FILE__, __LINE__, __VA_
ARGS__)

extern void SetupNativeLogging(const char * logFileName);
extern void CloseNativeLogging();

#endif // __NATIVE_LOGGING_H__
```

Now, we need to fill out each of these functions, beginning with
`SetupNativeLogging`:

```
void SetupNativeLogging(const char * logFileName)
{
    /* Boiler plate init Python */
    Py_Initialize();

    /* Init our config module into Python memory */
    initPythonLoggingBackend();

    /* call directly into our cython module  */
    initLoggingWithLogFile(logFileName);
}
```

This function is responsible for initializing Python and the Python logging
backend module. This is equivalent to an `import` statement in Python but
because we are in the driving seat in C we must load it natively. As well as its
respective `initLoggingWithLogFile` so that the logger will output a log file.
We can implement a simple C `info`, `error`, and `debug` by using the `va_list`
and `vsprintf` family of functions to turn the argument list and format into
a C string ready to print:

```
void native_logging_info(const char * file, unsigned line, const char
* fmt, ...)
{
```

```
    char buffer[256];
    va_list args;
    va_start(args, fmt);
    vsprintf(buffer, fmt, args);
    va_end(args);

// append file/line information
    char buf[512];
    snprintf(buf, sizeof(buf), "%s:%i -> %s", file, line, buffer);

// call python logging.info
    python_info(buf);
}
```

Now that we have these macros calling their respective log functions within C, we simply need to define the CloseNativeLogging, which is simple as we just need to close down Python:

```
void CloseNativeLogging()
{
    /* cleanup python before exit ... */
    Py_Finalize();
}
```

By wiring all this up together, we have a very nice way of using Python within C/C++, as if it was nothing strange:

```
#include "NativeLogging.h"

int main(int argc, char **argv)
{
    // we want to ensure we use a command line argument for the output
log file
    if (argc < 2) {
        return -1;
    }

    // use the first argument as log file
    SetupNativeLogging(argv[1]);

    // log out some stuff at different levels
    info("info message");
    debug("debug message");
    error("error message");
```

```
    // close up everything including Python
    CloseNativeLogging();

    return 0;
}
```

Note that this is the fully embedded link model for Cython. I decided to wrap all Python-specific code within the implementation. It's very easy to see how you could even migrate from using an old legacy logging API to using Python logging to get access to the massive feature set available, such as logging, to a network socket.

Running this example, we can see the output as we would expect:

```
$ cd chapter2/PythonLogging
$ make
$ ./example output.log
$ cat output.log
INFO 10/25/2015 07:04:45: main.c:14 -> info message
ERROR 10/25/2015 07:04:45: main.c:15 -> debug message
DEBUG 10/25/2015 07:04:45: main.c-16 -> error message
```

What's really nice here is that we have been able to preserve the line information from C/C++ all the way into the Python code. This example used the function wrapping concepts as well as the embedded linking model. No special programming tricks were used in this example.

Using Python ConfigParser from C/C++

I really like Python's ConfigParser API. I find using an INI style config file to be very readable and nice to work with as opposed to using XML or JSON. There are very few cross-platform libraries available to do this. However, when you have Cython, all you need is Python.

For this example, we will create a sample INI configuration file and write a simple API to access a list of sections, list of keys available in a section, and a way to get the value from a specified key within a section. These three functions will allow a programmer to access any INI file.

A sample INI file could be:

```
[example]
number = 15
path = some/path/to/something

[another_section]
test = something
```

An INI file is comprised of sections within the square brackets, followed by keys and values. It's a very simple way of doing configuration. Python's API allows for variables and substitution depending on the flavor of the ConfigParser. Firstly, we need a way to query the list of sections within an INI file:

```
from ConfigParser import SafeConfigParser
from libc.stdlib cimport malloc

cdef public struct ConfigSections:
    size_t number_of_sections
    char ** sections

cdef public void ParseSectionsFromConfig(const char *config_path,
ConfigSections * const sections):
    parser = SafeConfigParser()
    with open(config_path) as config_fd:
        try:
            parser.readfp(config_fd)
            sectionsInConfig = parser.sections()
            sections.number_of_sections = len(sectionsInConfig)
            sections.sections = <char **>malloc(sections.number_of_
sections)
            for i in range(sections.number_of_sections):
                sections.sections[i] = sectionsInConfig[i]
        except:
            sections.number_of_sections = 0
            sections.sections = NULL
```

There are a few things going on here to take note of. Firstly, the following:

```
cdef public struct ConfigSections
```

This public struct declaration, as we have seen before, will be the output into the respective header file. This means we don't have to define this inside the C/C++ code first:

```
cdef public void ParseSectionsFromConfig(const char *config_path,
ConfigSections * const sections):
```

This function is designed to take the path to the configuration file as a string. It also takes the pointer to the struct ConfigSections. This ConfigSections structure allows us to return a list of sections back into C code safely. C is a very simple language and does not have any nice variable length structures like C++'s STL library.

So, we must return a pointer to a list of C-Strings and the number of strings in that list. Since this structure is passed as an argument, the Cython code does not have to allocate and return a pointer, which is less efficient and not a standard C approach for small structures such as this. Note that we do have to allocate the list of strings:

```
sections.sections = <char **>malloc(sections.number_of_sections)
```

As with C++, Cython code requires an explicit cast when allocating memory with malloc. We will review this cast syntax later for more advanced usage. Next, we need to implement:

```
cdef public void ParseKeysFromSectionFromConfig(const char * config_
path, const char * section, ConfigSectionKeys * keys):
```

And finally, to get values from keys within sections:

```
cdef public char * ParseConfigKeyFromSection(const char *config_path,
const char * section, const char * key):
```

Now that we have all these functions, we can write C code to iterate over the sections in any given config file, and print everything out programmatically to demonstrate how powerful this can be:

```c
#include "PythonConfigParser.h"

static
void print_config(const char * config_file)
{
    struct ConfigSections sections;
    ParseSectionsFromConfig(config_file, &sections);

    size_t i;
    for (i = 0; i < sections.number_of_sections; ++i) {
        const char *current_section = sections.sections[i];
        printf("[%s]\n", current_section);

        struct ConfigSectionKeys sectionKeys;
        ParseKeysFromSectionFromConfig(config_file, current_section,
&sectionKeys);

        size_t j;
        for (j = 0; j < sectionKeys.number_of_keys; ++j) {
            const char * current_key = sectionKeys.keys[j];
            char *key_value = ParseConfigKeyFromSection(config_file,
current_section, current_key);
```

```
            printf("%s = %s\n", current_key, key_value);
        }
        free(sectionKeys.keys);
    }
    free(sections.sections);
}
```

Using the technique of passing reference to allocated structs on the stack, we eliminate a lot of memory management, but because we allocated memory to the arrays within each struct, we must free them. But note that we can simply return the value for ParseConfigKeyFromSection:

```
cdef public char * ParseConfigKeyFromSection(const char *config_path,
const char * section, const char * key):
    parser = SafeConfigParser()
    with open(config_path) as config_fd:
        try:
            parser.readfp(config_fd)
            return parser.get(section, key)
        except:
            return NULL
```

When returning C strings from Cython functions, we do not need to free anything, as this is managed by the Python garbage collector. It feels very strange to be able to return strings like this from Cython, but it's perfectly fine to do so.

Running this example, we can see:

```
$ cd Chapter2/PythonConfigParser
$ make
$ ./example sample.cfg
[example]
number = 15
path = some/path/to/something
[another_section]
test = something
```

You can see that we successfully parsed out all sections, keys, and values from the INI file programmatically.

Callbacks from Python to C/C++

Callbacks are used extensively in asynchronous systems. Libraries such as libevent provide a powerful asynchronous core to process events. Let's build an example to set a C function as a callback into a Python backend, which will notify back again into the C code. Firstly, we will declare a public callback function `typedef`:

```
cdef public:
    ctypedef void (*callback)(int)
```

This will output a callback `typedef`. Next, we can declare a global callback on the stack:

```
cdef callback GlobalCallback
```

Once this is set, we can then notify the `callback` easily. Next, we need a way to set the `callback` and another to call the `callback`:

```
cdef public void SetCallback(callback cb):
    global GlobalCallback
    GlobalCallback = cb
```

Notice the `global` keyword from Python through which the compiler knows to use the `global` keyword and not create a temporary instance from within that suite:

```
cdef public void Notify(int value):
    global GlobalCallback
    if GlobalCallback != <callback>0:
        GlobalCallback(value)
```

The `Notify` will take an argument and pass this argument to the callback. Again, we need to use the `global` keyword to ensure that the compiler will use the proper `global` keyword. Using the cast again, we ensure that we can never call a null `callback`. Next, we need to declare a `callback` inside the C code:

```
static
void MyCallback(int val)
{
    printf("[MYCALLBACK] %i\n", val);
}
```

Then, we can set the `callback`:

```
SetCallback(&MyCallback);
```

And finally, `Notify`:

```
Notify(12345);
```

This is the output we should expect:

```
$ cd Chapter2/PythonCallbacks
$ make
$ ./example
[MYCALLBACK] 12345
```

Later, we will use this more extensively to produce a simple Python message broker.

Cython PXD

The use of PXD files is very similar to that of header files in C/C++. When writing bindings to any C/C++ code, it is a good practice to declare all C/C++ interfaces within a `.pxd` file. This stands for **Python External Declarations**, at least it does in my mind. So, when we add blocks such as this:

```
cdef extern from "AddFunction.h":
    cdef int AddFunction(int, int)
```

We can instead put this directly into a `bindings.pxd` file and import this at any time inside any `.pyx` file:

```
cimport bindings
```

Notice the distinction between `cimport` for the `.pxd` files and a simple import for all normal Python imports.

> Cython's input filenames cannot handle dashes (`-`) in their filenames. It's best to try and use CamelCase, since you can't use `cimport my-import` in Python.

Integration with build systems

This topic is basically dependent on the linking model that you choose if you are to choose the shared-library approach. I would recommend using Python `distutils` and if you are going for embedded Python, and if you like GNU or autotools, this section gives an example you can use.

Python Distutils

When compiling a native Python module, we can use `distutils` and `cythonize` inside our `Setup.py` build. It's the preferred way in Python to use Cython as part of the build:

```
from distutils.core import setup
from Cython.Build import cythonize

setup(
    ext_modules = cythonize("sourcecode.pyx")
)
```

This build file will support whichever version of Python you invoke the script with. When you run the build, your output will be of the same name of the input source code as a shared module in this case `sourcecode.so`.

GNU/Autotools

To embed Python code within C/C++ applications using the autotools build system the following snippet will help you. It will use `python-config` to get the compiler and linker flags necessary to do so:

```
found_python=no
AC_ARG_ENABLE(
        python,
        AC_HELP_STRING(--enable-python, create python support),
        found_python=yes
)
AM_CONDITIONAL(IS_PYTHON, test "x%found_python" = xyes)

PYLIBS=""
PYINCS=""
if test "x$found_python" = xyes; then
   AC_CHECK_PROG(CYTHON_CHECK,cython,yes)
   if test x"$CYTHON_CHECK" != x"yes" ; then
     AC_MSG_ERROR([Please install cython])
   fi
   AC_CHECK_PROG(PYTHON_CONF_CHECK,python-config,yes)
   PYLIBS=`python-config --libs`
   PYINCS=`python-config --includes`
   if test "x$PYLIBS" == x; then
     AC_MSG_ERROR("python-dev not found")
   fi
fi
AC_SUBST(PYLIBS)
AC_SUBST(PYINCS)
```

This adds the `--enable-python` switch to your configure script. You now have the Cython command `found` and the `PYLIBS` and `PYINCS` variables for the compilation flags you need to compile. Now, you need a snippet to understand how to compile `*.pyx` in your sources in automake:

```
bin_PROGRAMS = myprog
ACLOCAL_AMFLAGS = -I etc
CFLAGS += -I$(PYINCS)

LIBTOOL_DEPS = @LIBTOOL_DEPS@
libtool: $(LIBTOOL_DEPS)
        $(SHELL) ./config.status libtool

SUFFIXES = .pyx
.pyx.c:
        @echo "   CPY   " $<
        @cython -2 -o $@ $<

myprog_SOURCES = \
        src/bla.pyx \
...
myprog_LDADD = \
        $(PYLIBS)
```

When you're comfortable with understanding where your code is and the linking models, embedding Python becomes very easy.

Summary

There are a lot of fundamentals of using Cython in this chapter. It's important to review what you want to achieve when using Cython, since the different ways in which it can be used affects how you design a solution. We investigated the differences between `def`, `cdef`, and `cpdef`. We created public C/C++ declarations of types and callable functions. Using these public declarations, we showed how Python can callback into C code. For me, reusing any Python module within native code is very useful and interesting. I demonstrated how I use the Python `logging` and `ConfigParser` modules from C code. Appreciating these simple examples, we will see how we can extend C/C++ projects with Python code in the next chapter.

3
Extending Applications

As mentioned in previous chapters, I want to show you how to interact or extend existing code using Cython. So, let's get right to doing that. Cython was originally designed to make raw Python computation faster. So, the initial proof of concept for Cython was to enable programmers to take existing Python code and use Cython's `cdef` keyword to require native typing to bypass the Python runtime for heavy computation. The culmination of this is increased performance in the time it takes to perform calculations and lower memory usage. It's even possible to write type-safe wrappers to existing Python libraries for fully typed Python code.

In this chapter, we will first see an example of typing Python code. Next, I will demonstrate the Cython `cdef` class, which allow us to wrap native C/C++ types into garbage collected Python classes. We will also see how to extend the native application **Tmux** with Python code by creating a pure Python command object, which is directly embedded into the native code.

In this chapter, we will cover the following topics:

- Cython pure Python code
- Compiling pure Python code
- Python garbage collector
- Extending Tmux
- Embedding Python
- Cythonzing struct cmd_entry
- Implementing a Tmux command

Cython pure Python code

Let's view a mathematical application that is actually taken from the Cython documentation. I wrote this equivalent in pure Python so that we can compare the speed. If you open the `primes` example for this chapter, you will see two programs—the Cython `primes.pyx` example, and my pure Python port. They both look almost the same:

```python
def primes(kmax):
    n = 0
    k = 0
    i = 0
    if kmax > 1000:
        kmax = 1000
    p = [0] * kmax
    result = []
    k = 0
    n = 2
    while k < kmax:
        i = 0
        while i < k and n % p[i] != 0:
            i = i + 1
        if i == k:
            p[k] = n
            k = k + 1
            result.append(n)
        n = n + 1
    return result
primes (10000)
```

This really is a direct Python port of that Cython code. Both call `primes (10000)`, but the evaluation time is very different between them in terms of performance:

```
$ make
cython --embed primes.pyx
gcc -g -O2 -c primes.c -o primes.o `python-config --includes`
gcc -g -O2 -o primes primes.o `python-config –libs`
$ time python pyprimes.py
        0.18 real          0.17 user          0.01 sys
$ time ./primes
        0.04 real          0.03 user          0.01 sys
```

You can see that the pure Python version was almost five times slower in doing the exact same job. Moreover, nearly every line of code is the same. Cython can do this because we have explicitly expressed the C types, hence there is no type conversion or folding, and we don't even have to use the Python runtime. I want to draw attention to the kind of speedups you can get with just simple code without calling into other native libraries. This is what makes Cython so prevalent in SAGE.

Compiling pure Python code

Another use for Cython is to compile Python code. For example, if we go back to the `primes` example, we can do the following:

```
$ cython pyprimes.py —embed
$ gcc -g -O2 pyprimes.c -o pyprimes `python-config --includes —libs`
```

Then, we can compare the three different versions of the same program: the Cython version using `cdef` for native types, the pure Python version running as a Python script, and finally, the Cython-compiled pure Python version, which results in an executable binary of Python code:

- First, the Cython version using native types:

```
$ time ./primes
real    0m0.050s
user    0m0.035s
sys     0m0.013s
```

- Next, the executable pure Python version:

```
$ time ./pyprimes
real    0m0.139s
user    0m0.122s
sys     0m0.013s
```

- And finally, the Python script version:

```
philips-macbook:primes redbrain$ time python pyprimes.py
real    0m0.184s
user    0m0.165s
sys     0m0.016s
```

The pure Python version runs the slowest, the compiled Python version runs a little bit faster, and finally, the natively-typed Cython version runs the fastest. I think it just draws attention to how well Cython can give you some dynamic language optimizations in several different ways.

Notice that when compiling the Python version to a binary, I specified –embed on invoking the Cython compiler. This tells the compiler to **--embed** a main method for us and to run as you would expect a normal Python script to run.

Avoid Makefiles – pyximport

From the previous example, you can see that it was code which didn't depend on any outside libraries. To make such code useful, wouldn't it be nice if we could bypass the Makefile and the invocation of compilers? It turns out that, in cases where we do not require linking against other native libraries, we can directly import our .pyx files into Python programs. You are required, however, to have Cython installed as a dependency.

Going back to *Chapter 1, Cython Won't Bite*, we can simply import our helloworld. pyx by importing pyximport first:

```
>>> import pyximport
>>> pyximport.install()
(None, <pyximport.pyximport.PyxImporter object at 0x102fba4d0>)
>>> import helloworld
Hello World from cython!
```

Behind the scenes, Cython is invoking all the compiler work for you so that you don't have to. But this leads to interesting ideas, such as that you could simply add Cython code to any Python project so long as Cython is a dependency.

Python garbage collector

When wrapping up native structs, for example, it can be very tempting to follow standard C/C++ idioms and require the Python programmer to call, allocate, and release manually on different objects. This is very tedious and not very Pythonic. Cython allows us to create cdef classes, which have extra hooks for initialization and deallocation that we can use to control all memory management of structs. These hooks are triggered automatically by the Python garbage collector, making everything nice and simple. Consider the following simple struct:

```
typedef struct data {
  int value;
} data_t;
```

We can then write the Cython declaration of the C `struct` into `PyData.pxd` as follows:

```
cdef extern from "Data.h":
    struct data:
        int value
    ctypedef data data_t
```

Now that we have defined the `struct`, we can wrap up the `struct` into a class:

```
cimport PyData

cdef class Data(object):
    cdef PyData.data_t * _nativeData
    ...
```

Wrapping up data into a class like this will require us to allocate and deallocate memory at the right moments. Thankfully, Cython exposes almost all of the `libc` as imports:

```
from libc.stdlib cimport malloc, free
```

Now that we can allocate memory and free it, all that is left is to understand the lifecycle of classes and where to hook into. Cython classes provide two special methods: `__cinit__` and `__dealloc__`. The `__cinit__` provides a way of instantiating native code, so for our case, we will allocate memory to the native C struct, and as you can guess on deallocate this is the destroy hook from the garbage collector and gives us a chance to free any allocated resources:

```
def __cinit__(self):
    self._nativeData = <data_t*>malloc(sizeof(data_t))
    if not self._nativeData:
        self._nativeData = NULL
        raise MemoryError()

def __dealloc__(self):
    if self._nativeData is not NULL:
        free(self._nativeData)
        self._nativeData = NULL
```

It's important to note that __cinit__ doesn't override Python __init__, and more importantly, __cinit__ is not designed to call into any Python code at this point as it does not guarantee full initialization of the class. An init method might look as follows:

```
def __init__(self, int value):
        self.SetValue(value)

def SetValue(self, int value):
        self.SetNativeValue(value)

cdef SetNativeValue(self, int value):
        self._nativeData.value = value
```

Note that we were able to type the arguments on these functions to ensure that we don't try and put a Python object into the struct, which would fail. What is impressive here is that this class behaves as if it was just a normal Python class:

```
from PyData import Data

def TestPythonData():
    # Looks and feels like normal python objects
    objectList = [Data(1), Data(2), Data(3)]

    # Print them out
    for dataObject in objectList:
        print dataObject

    # Show the Mutability
    objectList[1].SetValue(1234)
    print objectList[1]
```

If you put a simple print statement on the __dealloc__ hook and run the program, you will see all destructors are executed, as you would expect. It means we have just leveraged the Python garbage collector on top of native code.

Extending Tmux

Tmux is a terminal multiplexer inspired by GNU Screen (http://tmux.github.io/), but it supports much simpler and better configuration. More importantly, the implementation is much cleaner and easier to maintain, and it also uses libevent and very well-written C code.

I want to show you how you can extend Tmux with new built-in commands by writing Python code instead of C. Overall, there are several parts to this project, as follows:

- Hack the autotool's build system to compile in Cython
- Create PXD declarations to the relevant declarations such as `struct cmd_entry`
- Embed Python into Tmux
- Add the Python command to the global Tmux `cmd_table`

Let's take a quick look at the Tmux source, and in particular any of the `cmd-*.c` files that contain command declarations and implementations. Consider, for example, that `cmd-kill-window.c` is the command entry. This tells Tmux the name of the command, its alias, and how it may or may not accept arguments; finally, it accepts a function pointer to the actual command code:

```
const struct cmd_entry cmd_kill_window_entry = {
    "kill-window", "killw",
    "at:", 0, 0,
    "[-a] " CMD_TARGET_WINDOW_USAGE,
    0,
    NULL,
    NULL,
    cmd_kill_window_exec
};
```

So, if we are able to implement and initialize our own `struct` containing this information, we can run our `cdef` code. Next, we need to look at how Tmux picks up this command definition and how it gets executed.

If we look at `tmux.h`, we find the prototypes for everything that we need to manipulate:

```
extern const struct cmd_entry *cmd_table[];
extern const struct cmd_entry cmd_attach_session_entry;
extern const struct cmd_entry cmd_bind_key_entry;
....
```

So, we need to add a prototype here for our cmd_entry definition. Next, we need to look at cmd.c; this is where the command table is initialized so that it can be looked up later on to execute commands:

```
const struct cmd_entry *cmd_table[] = {
  &cmd_attach_session_entry,
  &cmd_bind_key_entry,
...
```

Now that the command table is initialized, where does the code get executed? If we look at the cmd_entry definition in the tmux.h header, we can see the following:

```
/* Command definition. */
struct cmd_entry {
  const char  *name;
  const char  *alias;

  const char  *args_template;
  int         args_lower;
  int         args_upper;

  const char  *usage;

#define CMD_STARTSERVER 0x1
#define CMD_CANTNEST 0x2
#define CMD_SENDENVIRON 0x4
#define CMD_READONLY 0x8
  int         flags;

  void        (*key_binding)(struct cmd *, int);
  int         (*check)(struct args *);
  enum cmd_retval  (*execc)(struct cmd *, struct cmd_q *);
};
```

The execc hook is the function pointer we really care about, so if you grep the sources, you should find the following:

```
Philips-MacBook:tmux-project redbrain$ ack-5.12 execc
tmux-1.8/cmd-queue.c
229:            retval = cmdq->cmd->entry->execc(cmdq->cmd, cmdq);
```

You might notice that in the official Tmux Git, this hook is simply named exec. I renamed this to execc because exec is a reserved word in Python—we need to avoid things like that. To begin with, let's get some code compiled. First, we need to get the build system to play ball.

Tmux build system

Tmux uses autotools, so we can reuse the snippets from *Chapter 2, Understanding Cython*, to add in Python support. We can add the –enable-python switch into configure.ac as follows:

```
# want python support for pytmux scripting
found_python=no
AC_ARG_ENABLE(
   python,
   AC_HELP_STRING(--enable-python, create python support),
   found_python=yes
)
AM_CONDITIONAL(IS_PYTHON, test "x$found_python" = xyes)

PYLIBS=""
PYINCS=""
if test "x$found_python" = xyes; then
   AC_CHECK_PROG(CYTHON_CHECK,cython,yes)
   if test x"$CYTHON_CHECK" != x"yes" ; then
      AC_MSG_ERROR([Please install cython])
   fi
   AC_CHECK_PROG(PYTHON_CONF_CHECK,python-config,yes)
   PYLIBS=`python-config --libs`
   PYINCS=`python-config --includes`
   if test "x$PYLIBS" == x; then
      AC_MSG_ERROR("python-dev not found")
   fi
   AC_DEFINE(HAVE_PYTHON)
fi
AC_SUBST(PYLIBS)
AC_SUBST(PYINCS)
```

This gives us the ./configure --enable-python option. Next, we need to look at the Makefile.am file. Let's call our Cython file cmdpython.pyx. Note that Cython doesn't like awkward characters such as "-" in the filename, as explained in *Chapter 2, Understanding Cython*. If we are to make Python support a conditional option at build time, we should add the following to Makefile.am:

```
if IS_PYTHON
PYTHON_SOURCES = cmdpython.pyx
else
PYTHON_SOURCES =
endif
```

```
# List of sources.
dist_tmux_SOURCES = \
  $(PYTHON_SOURCES) \
...
```

We have to make sure that it is needed and compiled first. Remember that if we create public declarations, Cython generates a header for us. We will simply add our public header to tmux.h to keep headers very simple. Then, to make sure Cython files get picked up by automake and is compiled properly according to the correct dependency management at build time, we need to add the following:

```
SUFFIXES = .pyx
.pyx.c:
  @echo " CPY    " $<
  @cython -2 -o $@ $<
```

This adds in the suffix rule to make sure the *.pyx files are Cythoned and then told to compile the resulting .c file just as any normal C file. This snippet plays well if you happen to use AM_SILENT_RULES([yes]) in your autotools project, which formats the echo message correctly. Lastly, we need to make sure we add the necessary CFLAGS and LIBS options to the compiler from AC_SUBST in the configure script:

```
CFLAGS += $(PYINCS)
tmux_LDADD = \
  $(PYLIBS)
```

Now you should have everything ready in the build system, but we have to regenerate the autotools stuff now because of the changes made. Simply run ./autogen.sh.

Embedding Python

Now that we have files being compiled, we need to initialize Python. Our module. Tmux is a forked server that clients connect to, so try not to think of it as a single-threaded system. It's a client *and* a server, so all commands are executed on the server. Now, let's find where the event loop is started in the server, and initialize and finalize the server here so that it's done correctly. Looking at int server_start(int lockfd, char *lockfile), we can add the following:

```
#ifdef HAVE_PYTHON
  Py_InitializeEx (0);
#endif
  server_loop ();
```

```
#ifdef HAVE_PYTHON
  Py_Finalize ();
#endif
```

Python is now embedded into the Tmux server. Notice that instead of using simply `Py_Initialize`, I used `Py_InitializeEx (0)`. This replicates the same behavior, but doesn't start up normal Python signal handlers. Tmux has its own signal handlers, so I don't want to override them. It's probably a good idea when extending established applications such as this to use `Py_InitializeEx (0)`, since they generally implement their own signal handling. Using this stops Python from trying to handle signals that would conflict.

Cythonizing struct cmd_entry

Next, let's consider creating a `cythonfile.pxd` file for the necessary `cdef` declarations of Tmux that we need to be aware of. We need to look at the `struct cmd_entry` declaration, and work backwards from this:

```
struct cmd_entry {
  const char  *name;
  const char  *alias;

  const char  *args_template;
  int      args_lower;
  int      args_upper;

  const char  *usage;
  int      flags;

  void      (*key_binding)(struct cmd *, int);
  int      (*check)(struct args *);
  enum cmd_retval    (*execc)(struct cmd *, struct cmd_q *);
};
```

As you can see, `cmd_entry` depends on several other types, so we need to work backwards a little bit. If you're going to be lazy and live dangerously, you can get away with it sometimes if you don't care about accessing the data correctly by casting any pointers such as `void *`. But if you're a seasoned C programmer, you know this is fairly dangerous and should be avoided. You can see this type depends on `struct cmd *`, `struct cmd_q *`, and `struct args *`. We would ideally want to access these at some point, so it's a good idea to work backwards and implement them one at a time, since the rest are just native C types, which Cython understands.

Implementing the `enum` should be by far the simplest:

```
/* Command return values. */
enum cmd_retval {
  CMD_RETURN_ERROR = -1,
  CMD_RETURN_NORMAL = 0,
  CMD_RETURN_WAIT,
  CMD_RETURN_STOP
};
```

Then, turn it into the following:

```
cdef enum cmd_retval:
        CMD_RETURN_ERROR = -1
        CMD_RETURN_NORMAL = 0
        CMD_RETURN_WAIT = 1
        CMD_RETURN_STOP = 2
```

Now that we have the return value for the `exec` hook, we need to look at `struct cmd` next and implement it:

```
struct cmd {
  const struct cmd_entry  *entry;
  struct args     *args;

  char        *file;
  u_int       line;

  TAILQ_ENTRY(cmd)    qentry;
};
```

Take a look at `TAILQ_ENTRY`. This is simply a preprocessor macro that is a **BSD libc** extension to turn any type into its own linked list. We can ignore this:

```
cdef struct cmd:
        cmd_entry * entry
        args * aargs
        char * file
        int line
```

Note that this `struct` depends on the `struct cmd_entry` and `struct args` definitions, which we haven't implemented yet. Don't worry about this yet; just put them in for now. Next, let's implement `struct args`, since it's simple:

```
/* Parsed arguments. */
struct args {
  bitstr_t  *flags;
```

```
char      *values[SCHAR_MAX];

int       argc;
char          **argv;
};
```

Note that it uses `bitstr_t` and a variable-length array list. I choose to ignore `bitstr_t` because I think it's a system-dependent header that is fairly tricky to implement. Let's simply cast these as `char *` and `char **` to get things working:

```
cdef struct args:
        char * flags
        char **values
        int argc
        char **argv
```

Now that the `args` structure is Cythonized, let's implement `struct cmd_q`, which is a little trickier:

```
/* Command queue. */
struct cmd_q {
    int        references;
    int        dead;

    struct client    *client;
    int        client_exit;

    struct cmd_q_items    queue;
    struct cmd_q_item  *item;
    struct cmd     *cmd;

    time_t        time;
    u_int         number;

    void          (*emptyfn)(struct cmd_q *);
    void        *data;

    struct msg_command_data   *msgdata;

    TAILQ_ENTRY(cmd_q)        waitentry;
};
```

There are quite a few more structs that this depends on, but we will not see them here. Let's try and cast these for now; for example, `struct client *`. We can cast this as `void *`, and then `struct cmd_q_items` simply as `int`, even though it isn't correct. As long as we are not going to try and access these fields, we will be okay. But remember that if we were to use Cython `sizeof`, we could run into memory corruption with different sizes allocated by C and by Cython. We can work down the other types such as `struct cmd_q_item *` and cast them as `void *` again. Finally, we come to `time_t`, where we can reuse `libc.stdlib` `cimport` time from Cython. This is a really good exercise to implement Cython declarations for C applications; it really exercises your code analysis. When going through really long structures, remember that we can get things going by just casting them as `void`. Be careful about the `struct` alignment and typing if you care about the data types in your Cython API:

```
cdef struct cmd_q:
        int references
        int dead
        void * client
        int client_exit
        int queue
        void * item
        cmd * cmd
        int time
        int number
        void (*emptyfn)(cmd_q *)
        void * msgdata
```

That was a fairly deep dive into a lot of project-specific internals, but I hope you get the idea—we really didn't do anything terribly scary. We even cheated and casted things that we really don't care about. With all these auxiliary types implemented, we can finally implement the type we care about, namely, `struct cmd_entry`:

```
cdef struct cmd_entry:
        char * name
        char * alias
        char * args_template
        int args_lower
        int args_upper
        char * usage
        int flags
        void (*keybinding)(cmd *, int)
        int (*check)(args *)
        cmd_retval (*execc)(cmd *, cmd_q *)
```

With this `cmdpython.pxd` file, we can now implement our Tmux command!

Implementing a Tmux command

One caveat with Cython is that we cannot statically initialize structs like we can in C, so we need to make a hook so that we can initialize cmd_entry on Python startup:

```
cimport cmdpython

cdef public cmd_entry cmd_entry_python
```

With this, we now have a public declaration of cmd_entry_python, which we will initialize in a startup hook as follows:

```
cdef public void tmux_init_cython () with gil:
    cmd_entry_python.name = "python"
    cmd_entry_python.alias = "py"
    cmd_entry_python.args_template = ""
    cmd_entry_python.args_lower = 0
    cmd_entry_python.args_upper = 0
    cmd_entry_python.usage = "python usage..."
    cmd_entry_python.flags = 0
    #cmd_entry_python.key_binding = NULL
    #cmd_entry_python.check = NULL
    cmd_entry_python.execc = python_exec
```

Remember that because we declared this in the top level, we know it's on the heap and don't need to declare any memory to the structure, which is very handy for us. You've seen struct access before; the function suite should look familiar. But let me draw attention to a few things here:

- We declared public to make sure we can call it.
- The execution hook is simply a cdef Cython function.
- Finally, you might notice the gil. I will explain what this is used for in *Chapter 5, Advanced Cython*.

Now, let's see a simple execution hook:

```
cdef cmd_retval python_exec (cmd * cmd, cmd_q * cmdq) with gil:
    cdef char * message = "Inside your python command inside tmux!!!"
    log_debug (message)
    return CMD_RETURN_NORMAL;
```

There is not much left to do to hook this into Tmux now. It simply needs to be added to cmd_table and the startup hook needs to be added to the server initialization.

Note that I added something in the log_debug function to the
PXD; if you look into Tmux, this is a VA_ARGS function. Cython
doesn't understand these yet, but we can hack it just to get it going
by simply casting it as a function that takes a string. As long as we
don't try and use it like any printf, we should be fine.

Hooking everything together

We now have to fiddle with Tmux just a tiny bit more, but it's fairly painless,
and once we are done we are free to be creative. Fundamentally, we should call
the cmd_entry initialization hook in server.c just before we forget about it:

```
#ifdef HAVE_PYTHON
  Py_InitializeEx (0);
  tmux_init_cython ();
#endif


  server_loop();

#ifdef HAVE_PYTHON
  Py_Finalize ();
#endif
```

Now that this is done, we need to make sure we add the cmd_entry_python extern
declaration to tmux.h:

```
extern const struct cmd_entry cmd_wait_for_entry;
#ifdef HAVE_PYTHON
# include "cmdpython.h"
#endif
```

Finally, add this to cmd_table:

```
const struct cmd_entry *cmd_table[] = {
  &cmd_attach_session_entry,
  &cmd_bind_key_entry,
  &cmd_break_pane_entry,
...
  &cmd_wait_for_entry,
  &cmd_entry_python,
  NULL
};
```

Now that this is done, I think we're good to go—let's test out this baby. Compile Tmux with the following:

```
$ ./configure –enable-python
$ make
$ ./tmux -vvv
$ tmux: C-b :python
$ tmux: exit
```

We can look into `tmux-server-*.log` to see our debug message:

```
complete key ^M 0xd
cmdq 0xbb38f0: python (client 8)
Inside your python command inside tmux!!!
keys are 1 (e)
```

I hope you can now see how easily you can extend this to do something of your own choosing, such as using Python libraries to call directly into your music player, and it would all be integrated with Tmux.

Summary

There are many different techniques and ideas demonstrated in this chapter, but it should serve as a strong reference on common techniques. We saw the speedups in using native types to bypass the runtime, and compiled Python code into its own binary. The `pyximport` statement shows us we can bypass compilation and simply import `.pyx` files as if it was normal Python. Finally, I ended the chapter with a step-by-step demonstration of my process in embedding Python into Tmux. In the next chapter, we will see debugging in action using `gdb`, and some caveats in using Cython.

4
Debugging Cython

Since Cython programs compile down to their native code, we cannot use the Python debugger to step through your code. We can, however, use GDB. **GNU Project Debugger (GDB)** is a cross platform debugger. Python plugin support was added in version 7.0, which was used to add the Cython support into gdb as a simple script; this means that you can seamlessly step through the C/C++ code into Cython and back again.

When it comes to language binding, it's good practice to keep interfaces as simple as possible. This will make debugging much simpler until you are happy with your bindings in terms of resource management or stability. I will iterate over some GDB and caveats examples.

In this chapter, we will cover the following topics:

- Using GFB with Cython
- Cython caveats

Using GDB with Cython

To debug Cython, you need GDB >= 7.0. On Mac OS X Xcode, build tools have moved to LLVM and lldb as respective debuggers. You can install gdb using homebrew:

```
$ brew install gdb
```

We cannot use the Python debugger since the Cython code is compiled down to C/C++. Therefore, when debugging without the Cython plugin, you will be stepping through the generated C/C++ code, which won't be helpful as it won't understand the context of the Cython program.

Running cygdb

Cygdb is installed as a part of Cython and is a wrapper over GDB (it invokes GDB with arguments to set up the Cython plugin). Before you can debug the Cython code, we need to generate the debugging information. Just like C/C++, we need to specify compiler options to generated debuggable code we can pass –gdb when invoking the Cython compiler:

```
$ cython --gdb cycode.pyx
```

> Before you start debugging on Debian, you need to install the Python debug information package and GDB as it is not installed with `build-essential`. To install these, run the following:
>
> ```
> $ sudo apt-get install gdb build-essential
> cython python-dbg
> ```

Now that you have GDB and the debug information generated, you can start the Cython debugger with this:

```
$ cygdb . --args python-dbg main.py
```

Once you're familiar with GDB, you can simply use all of the normal gdb commands. However, the whole point of cygdb is that we can use Cython commands, which we will see in use here with an explanation:

```
(gdb) cy break
__init__                    cycode.foobar.__init__    cycode.foobar.print_me
cycode.func                 func                      print_me
```

If you tab autocomplete cy break, you will see a list of symbols to which you can set a Cython break point. Next, we need to get the program running and continue to our break points as follows:

```
(gdb) cy break func

    Function "__pyx_pw_6cycode_1func" not defined.
    Breakpoint 1 (__pyx_pw_6cycode_1func) pending.
```

Now that we have the break point set, we need to run the program:

```
(gdb) cy run
1    def func (int x):
```

Now that we have hit the declaration of the `func` function, we can continue and do some introspection as follows:

```
(gdb) cy globals
Python globals:
    __builtins__  = <module at remote 0x7ffff7fabb08>
    __doc__       = None
    __file__      = '$HOME/chapter4/gdb1/cycode.so'
    __name__      = 'cycode'
    __package__   = None
    __test__      = {}
    foobar        = <classobj at remote 0x7ffff7ee50b8>
    func          = <built-in function func>
C globals:
```

The `globals` command will show any of the global identifiers in the scope of the current frame, so we can see the `func` function and `classobj foobar`. We can inspect further by listing the code and step code:

```
(gdb) cy list
     1    def func (int x):
     2        print x
     3        return x + 1
     4
```

We can also step the code as follows:

```
(gdb) cy step
1
4    cycode.func (1)

(gdb) cy list
     1    #!/usr/bin/python
     2    import cycode
     3
     4    cycode.func (1)
>    5    object = cycode.foobar ()
     6    object.print_me ()

(gdb) cy step
3        return x + 1

(gdb) cy list
     1    def func (int x):
     2        print x
```

```
   >    3            return x + 1
        4
        5    class foobar:
        6        x = 0
        7        def __init__ (self):
```

You can get fairly neat listings even from classes:

```
(gdb) cy list
        3            return x + 1
        4
        5    class foobar:
        6        x = 0
        7        def __init__ (self):
   >    8            self.x = 1
        9
       10        def print_me (self):
       11            print self.x
```

We can even see the backtrace of the current Python state:

```
(gdb) cy bt
#9   0x000000000047b6a0 in <module>() at main.py:6
        6       object.print_me ()
#13 0x00007ffff6a05ea0 in print_me() at /home/redbrain/cython-book/
chapter4/gdb1/cycode.pyx:8
        8                 self.x = 1
```

The help can be found by running the following command:

```
(gdb) help cy
```

I think you have got the idea! It's worth playing around, checking the help, and trying these for yourself to get the feel of debugging with cygdb. To get a good feel, you really need to practice with GDB and get comfortable with it.

Cython caveats

There are some caveats worth noting while mixing C and the Python code when it comes to Cython. It's a good idea to refer to these when building something to be production ready.

Type checking

You may have noticed that in the previous code examples, we were able to cast the void * pointer from `malloc` to our extension types using `malloc`. Cython supports some more advanced type checking as follows:

```
char * buf = <char *> malloc (sizeof (...))
```

In basic type casting, Cython supports `<type?>` for type checking:

```
char * buf  = <char *?> malloc (...)
```

This will do some type checking and throw an error if the type that is being cast is not a subclass of char *. So, in this case, it will pass; however, if you were to do the following:

```
cdef class A:
    pass
cdef class B (A):
    pass

def myfunc ():
    cdef A class1 = A ()
    cdef B class2 = B ()
    cdef B x = <B?> class1
```

This will return an error (at runtime):

```
Traceback (most recent call last):
  File "main.py", line 2, in <module>
    myfunc ()
  File "cycode.pyx", line 12, in cycode.myfunc (cycode.c:714)
    cdef B x = <B?> class1
TypeError: Cannot convert cycode.A to cycode.B
```

So, this can add some more type safety to your Cython APIs.

Dereference operator (*)

In Cython, we don't have a dereference operator. For example, if you are passing a C array and length to a function, you can use pointer arithmetic to iterate and access elements of the array:

```
int * ptr = array;
int i;
for (i = 0; i < len; ++i)
  printf ("%i\n", *ptr++);
```

In Cython, we have to be a little more explicit by accessing element zero. Then, we increment the pointer:

```
cdef int i
cdef int * ptr = array
for i in range (len):
    print ptr [0]
    ptr = ptr + 1
```

There is nothing really fancy here. You simply have to use `x[0]` if you want to dereference `int *x`.

Python exceptions

Another topic to look at is what happens if your Cython code propagates an exception to your C code. In the next chapter, we will cover how C++ native exceptions interact with Python, but we do not have this in C. Consider the following code:

```
cdef public void myfunc ():
    raise Exception ("Raising an exception!")
```

This simply raises an exception back to C and gives the following:

```
$ ./test
Exception: Exception('Raising an exception!',) in 'cycode.myfunc'
ignored
Away doing something else now...
```

As you can see, a warning was printed and no exception handling had occurred, so the program continues onto something else. This is because the plain `cdef` functions that do not return Python objects have no way for exceptions to be handled; and thus, a simple warning message is printed. If we want to control the behavior for C programs, we need to declare the exception on the Cython function prototype.

There are three forms for doing this. First, we can do the following:

```
cdef int myfunc () except -1:
    cdef int retval = -1
    ....
    return retval
```

This makes the function throw an exception on the function returning `-1` at any point. This also causes the exception to be propagated to the caller; so, in Cython, we can do the following:

```
cdef public void run ():
    try:
        myfunc ()
        somethingElse ()
    except Exception:
        print "Something wrong"
```

You can also use the *maybe* exception (as I would like to think of it), which looks as follows:

```
cdef int myfunc () except ? -1:
    cdef int retval = -1
     ....
     return retval
```

This means that it may or may not be an error. Cython generates a call to `PyErr_Occurred` to perform verification from the C API. Lastly, we can use the wildcard:

```
cdef int myfunc () except *:
```

This then makes it always call `PyErr_Occurred`, which you can check via `PyErr_PrintEx` or via others at `http://docs.python.org/2/c-api/exceptions.html`.

Note that the function pointer declarations can also handle this in their prototype. Just make sure that the return type matches the exception type, which must be an enum, float, pointer-type, or constant expression; if this is not the case, you will get a confusing compilation error.

C/C++ iterators

Cython has more support for the C style `for` loops, and it can also perform further optimizations on the `range` function depending on how the iterator is declared. Generally, in Python, you simply do the following:

```
for i in iterable_type: ...
```

This is fine on PyObjects since they understand iterators, but C types do not have any of these abstractions. You need to do pointer arithmetic on your array types to access indexes. So, for example, first we can do the following with the `range` function:

```
cdef void myfunc (int length, int * array)
    cdef int i
    for i in range (length):
        print array [i]
```

When the range function is used on C types, such as the following example that uses `cdef int i`, it is optimized for real C array access. There are several other forms we can use. We could translate the loop into the following:

```
cdef int i
for i in array [:length]: print i
```

This looks a lot more like a normal Python `for` loop performing the iteration assigning `i`, the index data. There is also one last form that Cython introduces using the `for .. from` syntax. This looks like a real `for` loop from C, and we can now write:

```
def myfunc (int length, int * array):
    cdef int i
    for i from 0 <= i < length;
        print array [i]
```

We can also introduce the step size:

```
for i from 0 <= i < length by 2:
    print array [i]
```

These extra `for` loop constructs are particularly useful when working a lot with C types because they do not understand extra Python constructs.

Boolean error

When you try and use `bool` in Cython, you will get the following:

```
cycode.pyx:2:9: 'bool' is not a type identifier
```

So, you need to use this:

```
from libcpp cimport bool
```

When you compile it, you get the following:

```
cycode.c: In function '__pyx_pf_6cycode_run':
cycode.c:642: error: 'bool' undeclared (first use in this function)
cycode.c:642: error: (Each undeclared identifier is reported only once
cycode.c:642: error: for each function it appears in.)
cycode.c:642: error: expected ';' before '__pyx_v_mybool'
cycode.c:657: error: '__pyx_v_mybool' undeclared (first use in this
function)
```

You need to make sure you're compiling with a C++ compiler as `bool` is a native type.

Const keyword

Cython doesn't understand the `const` keyword pre Cython 0.18, but we can work around this with the following typedefs:

```
cdef extern from *:
    ctypedef char* const_char_ptr "const char*"
```

Now, we can use the `const` keyword as follows:

```
cdef public void foo_c(const_char_ptr s):
    ...
```

If you're using Cython greater than or equal to 0.18, you can use `const` just as you would from C.

Multiple Cython inputs

Cython does not handle multiple `.pyx` files. So, Cython has another keyword and convention— `.pxi`. This is an extra include file that works just as C includes. All other Cython files get pulled into one file to make one Cython compilation. For this, you need to do the following:

```
include "myothercythonfile.pxi"
```

It's important to remember that this works as a C include and will put in place the code from the file to the point of the include.

Struct initialization

When declaring `struct`, you cannot do normal C initialization as follows:

```
struct myStruct {
  int x;
  char * y;
}
struct myStruct x = { 2, "bla" };
```

You need to do the following:

```
cdef myStruct x:
x.x = 2
x.y = "bla"
```

So, you manually specify the fields more verbosely. So, when using structs, you should ensure to use memset or set each element explicitly before using it.

Calling into pure Python modules

You can always call into some pure Python code (non-Cythoned), but you should always beware and use Python `disutils` to make sure the module is installed correctly outside of the development environment.

Summary

Overall, we have seen some basic debugging using the cygdb wrapper. More importantly, we have examined some caveats and features of Cython. In the next chapter, we will see how we can bind C++ code and work with C++ constructs, such as templates and the STL library, in particular, directly from Cython. We will also see how the GIL can affect working with code in Cython and C/C++.

5
Advanced Cython

Throughout this book, we have exclusively been mixing C and Python together. In this chapter, we will delve into C++ and Cython. With every release of Cython C++, the support has improved. This is not to say that it's not ready for use yet. In this chapter, we will cover the following topics:

- Make native C++ classes callable from Python.
- Wrapping C++ namespaces and templates
- How exceptions can be propagated to and from C++ and Python
- C++ new and del keyword
- Operator overloading
- Cython gil and nogil keywords

We will wrap up this chapter by embedding a web server into a toy C++ messaging server.

Cython and C++

Cython, above all binding generators, works with C++ the most seamlessly. C++ has some complexity when writing bindings for it, such as calling conventions, templates, and classes. I find this exception handling to be a shining feature of Cython, and we will look at the examples of each.

Namespaces

I am introducing namespaces first because Cython uses namespaces as a way to reference C++ code within your module. Consider this C++ header with the following namespace:

```
#ifndef __MY_HEADER_H__
#define __MY_HEADER_H__

namespace mynamespace {
....
}

#endif //__MY_HEADER_H__
```

You will wrap this with the `cdef extern` declaration:

```
cdef extern from "header.h" namespace "mynamespace":
    ...
```

You can now address it in Cython as you normally would do for a module:

```
import cythonfile
cythonfile.mynamespace.attribute
```

It really feels like a Python module simply by using a namespace.

Classes

I would take a guess that most of your C++ code revolves around using classes. Being an object-oriented language, Cython handles this seamlessly:

```
#ifndef __MY_HEADER_H__
#define __MY_HEADER_H__

namespace mynamespace {
  void myFunc (void);

  class myClass {
  public:
    int x;
    void printMe (void);
  };
}

#endif //__MY_HEADER_H__
```

We can use Cython's `cppclass` keyword. This special keyword allows you to declare C++ classes and work with them directly, so you don't need to write the wrapper code, which can be very tedious and error prone in big projects. Using the previous namespace example, we will wrap the namespace and then the class within the namespace:

```
cdef extern from "myheader.h" namespace "mynamespace":
    void myFunc ()
    cppclass myClass:
        int x
        void printMe ()
```

It's pretty simple just as C types were. Though now, you have a native C++ object, which can be very powerful.

Remember that Cython will only care about the `public` attributes. Since these are the only attributes a callee can access due to the encapsulation of private and protected methods. It is not possible to extend the C++ class. Now, you can work with these as if they were just `cdef` structs. Just use the '.' operator as before to access all the necessary attributes.

C++ new and del keyword

Cython understands the `new` keyword from C++; so, consider that you have a C++ class:

```
class Car {
    int doors;
    int wheels;
  public:
    Car ();
    ~Car ();
    void printCar (void);
    void setWheels (int x) { wheels = x; };
    void setDoors (int x) { doors = x; };
};
```

It is defined in Cython as follows:

```
cdef extern from "cppcode.h" namespace "mynamespace":
    cppclass Car:
        Car ()
        void printCar ()
        void setWheels (int)
        void setDoors (int)
```

Note that we do not declare the `~Car` destructor because we never call this directly. It's not an explicitly callable public member; this is why we never call it directly but delete will and the compiler will ensure this is called when it will go out of scope on the stack. To instantiate the raw C++ class in Cython code on the heap, we can simply run the following:

```
cdef Car * c = new Car ()
```

You can then go and use `del` to delete the object at any time using Python's `del` keyword:

```
del c
```

You will see that the destructor is called as you would expect:

```
$ cd chapter5/cppalloc; make; ./test
Car constructor
Car has 3 doors and 4 wheels
Car destructor
```

We can also declare a stack-allocated object, but it must only have a default constructor such as the following:

```
cdef Car c
```

There is no way to pass arguments with this syntax in Cython. But, note that you cannot use `del` on this instance, else you will get the following error:

```
cpycode.pyx:13:6: Deletion of non-heap C++ object
```

Exceptions

With C++ exception handling, you can get a sense of how seamless Cython can feel within the C++ code. If any exceptions are thrown, such as memory allocations, Cython will handle these and translate them into more useful errors, and you still get the valid C++ exceptions objects. Python will also understand if these are caught or not and whether they are handled as required. This table gives you an idea of what Python exceptions will map to within C++:

C++	Python
bad_alloc	MemoryError
bad_cast	TypeError
domain_error	ValueError
invalid_argument	ValueError
ios_base::failure	IOError

out_of_range	IndexError
overflow_error	OverflowError
range_error	ArithmeticError
underflow_error	ArithmeticError
All other exceptions	RuntimeError

For instance, take this C++ code. It will simply throw an exception when the myFunc function is called. First, we define an exception with the following:

```
namespace mynamespace {
  class mycppexcept: public std::exception {
    virtual const char * what () const throw () {
      return "C++ exception happened";
    }
  };

  void myFunc (void) throw (mycppexcept);
}
```

Now, we write the function to throw the exception:

```
void mynamespace::myFunc (void) throw (mynamespace::mycppexcept) {
  mynamespace::mycppexcept ex;
  cout << "About to throw an exception!" << endl;
  throw ex;
}
```

We can call this in Cython with the following:

```
cdef extern from "myheader.h" namespace "mynamespace":
    void myFunc () except +RuntimeError
```

When we run the function, we get the following output:

```
>>> import cpycode
About to throw an exception!
Traceback (most recent call last):
  File "<stdin>", line 1, in <module>
  File "cpycode.pyx", line 3, in init cpycode (cpycode.cpp:763)
    myFunc ()
RuntimeError: C++ exception happened
>>> ^D
```

If you want to catch the C++ exception in your Python code, you can simply use it as normal:

```
try:
...
except RuntimeError:
...
```

Notice that we told Cython to cast any exceptions to `RuntimeError`. This is important to make sure you understand where and which interfaces can throw an exception. Unhanded exceptions look really ugly and can be harder to debug. Cython cannot assume much about the state at this point since compilers won't throw errors on potentially unhandled exceptions in C++ at the code level. If this happens, you will get the following as the no exception handler is ready:

```
$ cd chapter5/cppexceptions; make; python
Python 2.7.2 (default, Oct 11 2012, 20:14:37)
[GCC 4.2.1 Compatible Apple Clang 4.0 (tags/Apple/clang-418.0.60)] on
darwin
Type "help", "copyright", "credits" or "license" for more information.
>>> import cpycode
About to throw an exception!
Segmentation fault: 11
```

Bool type

As seen in the previous chapter, to use the native `bool` type from C++, you need to firstly import the following:

```
from libcpp cimport bool
```

Then, you can use `bool` as a normal `cdef`. If you want to use the pure PyObject `bool` type, you need to import the following:

```
from cpython cimport bool
```

You can then assign them with the normal `true` or `false` values.

Overloading

Since Python supports overloading to wrap C++ overload, just list the members as normal:

```
cdef foobar (int)
cdef foobar (int, int)
...
```

Cython understands that we are in C++ mode and can handle all the type conversion as normal. It's interesting that it can also handle an operator overload easily since it is just another hook! For example, let's take the `Car` class again and perform some operator overriding such as the following:

```
namespace mynamespace {
  class Car {
    int doors;
    int wheels;
  public:
    Car ();
    ~Car ();
    Car * operator+(Car *);
    void printCar (void);
    void setWheels (int x) { wheels = x; };
    void setDoors (int x) { doors = x; };
  };
};
```

Remember to add these operator-overloading class members to your Cythonized class; otherwise, your Cython will throw the following error:

```
Invalid operand types for '+' (Car *; Car *)
```

The Cython declaration of the operator overload looks as you expected:

```
cdef extern from "cppcode.h" namespace "mynamespace":
    cppclass Car:
        Car ()
        Car * operator+ (Car *)
        void printCar ()
        void setWheels (int)
        void setDoors (int)
```

Now, you can do the following:

```
cdef Car * ccc = c[0] + cc
ccc.printCar ()
```

This will then give us the following output on the command line:

```
$ cd chapter5/cppoverloading; make; ./test
Car constructor
Car constructor
Car has 3 doors and 4 wheels
Car has 6 doors and 8 wheels
```

```
inside operator +
Car constructor
Car has 9 doors and 12 wheels
```

Everything is handled as you would expect. This, for me, demonstrates the principle that inspired Guido to design Python classes.

Templates

Templates are supported in Cython. Though, for the sake of completeness, template meta-programming patterns don't wrap up correctly or fail to compile. This keeps getting better with every release, so take this comment with a pinch of salt.

C++ class templates work very well; we can implement a template called `LinkedList` as the following class:

```
cppclass LinkedList[T]:
        LinkedList ()
        void append (T)
        int getLength ()
...
```

Now, you can access the template type with the declaration called `T`. You can follow the rest of this code in `chapter5/cpptemplates`.

Static class member attribute

Sometimes, in classes, it's useful to have a static attribute such as the following:

```
namespace mynamespace {
  class myClass {
    public:
      static void myStaticMethod (void);
  };
}
```

In Cython, there is no support for this via a `static` keyword, but what you can do is tie this function to a namespace so that it becomes the following:

```
cdef extern from "header.h" namespace "mynamespace::myClass":
    void myStaticMethod ()
```

Now, you simply call this method as a global method in Cython.

Calling C++ functions – Caveat

When you write a code to call in a C++ function from C, you need to wrap the prototypes in the following:

```
extern "C" { … }
```

This allows you to call C++ prototypes because C won't understand a C++ class. With Cython, if you are telling your C output to call in C++ functions, you need to be careful about which compiler you are using or you need to write a new header to implement the minimal wrapper functions required to make the C++ calls.

Namespaces – Caveat

Cython seems to generally require a namespace to keep things nested, which you are already probably doing in your C++ code. Making PXD on non-namespaced code seems to make new declarations, meaning that you will get linking errors due to multiple symbols. The C++ support looks really good from these templates, and more metaprogramming idioms can be difficult to express in Cython. When polymorphism comes into play, it can be difficult to track down compilation errors. I would stress that you should keep your interfaces as simple as possible to perform debugging and to be more dynamic!

 Remember, when using Cython to generate C++, you need to specify -cplus, so it will default the cythonfile.cpp output. Pay attention to the extensions; I prefer to use .cc for my C++ code, so just be careful with your build system.

Python distutils

As usual, we can also use Python distutils, but you will need to specify the language so that the auxiliary C++ code required will be compiled by the correct compiler:

```
from distutils.core import setup
from Cython.Build import cythonize

setup (ext_modules = cythonize(
    "mycython.pyx",
    sources = ["mysource.cc"],
    language = "c++",
))
```

Now, you can compile your C++ code to your Python module.

Python threading and GIL

GIL stands for **Global Interpreter Lock**. What this means is when you link your program against `libpython.so` and use it, you really have the entire Python interpreter in your code. The reason this exists is to make concurrent applications really easy. In Python you can have two threads reading/writing to the same location and Python automatically handles all of this for you; unlike say in Java, where you need to specify that everything is under the GIL in Python. There are two things to consider when talking about the GIL and what it does—instruction atomicity and read/write lock.

Atomic instructions

Remember that Cython necessarily generates the C code to make it look similar to any Python module that you can import. So, what's happening under the hood is that it will generate all the code to acquire lock on the GIL so that it can manipulate Python objects at runtime. Let's consider two types of execution. Firstly, you have the C stack where it executes atomically as you would expect; it doesn't care about synchronization between threads—this is left up to the programmer. The other is Python where it's doing all of this synchronization for us. When you embed Python into your application manually using `Py_Initilize`, this is under the C execution. When it comes to calling something, such as `import sys` and `sys.uname`, in the Cython code that is called from C, the Python GIL schedules, and blocks multiple threads from calling this at the same time to be safe. This makes writing multithreaded Python code extremely safe. Any errors from writing to the same location at the same time can happen and be handled correctly instead of having to use **mutex's** on critical sections in C.

Read/write lock

The read/write lock is great because it is pretty rare for you in Python to need to care about semaphores or mutex's on data unless you want to synchronize different thread's access to a resource. The worst that can happen is for you to get into an inconsistent state in your program, but you won't crash in contrast to C/C++. Any read/write operation to the global dictionary is handled the way you would expect in Python.

Cython keywords

Okay, so how does this affect you and, more importantly, your code? It is important to know what way your code should and/or will execute in a concurrent manner. Without an understanding of this, your debugging will be confusing. There are times when the GIL gets in the way and can cause issues by blocking the execution of your C code from Python or vice versa. Cython allows us to control the GIL with the `gil` and `nogil` keywords, which is much simpler by wrapping this state for us:

Cython	Python
With gil	`PyGILState_Ensure ()`
With nogil	`PyGILState_Release (state)`

I find that it's easier to think of multithreading in Python in terms of blocking and nonblocking the execution. In the next example, we will examine the steps needed to embed a web server into a toy messaging server.

Messaging server

The messaging server is an example of something that would be highly concurrent; let's say we want to embed a web server into this to show the list of clients that are connected to the server. If you look at the flask, you can see how easily you can have a full web container in about eight lines of code.

The messaging server is asynchronous; therefore, it is callback based in C code. These callbacks can then call into Python roster object via Cython. Then, we can iterate over the roster dictionary to get online clients and simply return some JSON as a web service very easily reusing Python code and no need to write anything in C/C++.

It's important to note when embedding web servers is that they start a lot of threads. Calling the start web server function will block until it will exit, meaning if we start the web server first, we won't have the messaging server running concurrently. Also, due to the web-server function blocking, if I start it on a separate thread, it will never exit. Therefore, we are forced to run the messaging server on a background thread, and we can do this from the Python threading module. Again, this is where the GIL state becomes important. If we were to run the messaging server with the GIL and when the callbacks start, they will crash or block when they callback into Python. We can wrap the messaging server into the toy class called `MessageServer`:

```
class MessageServer(threading.Thread):

    _port = None
```

```python
    def __init__ (self, port):
        threading.Thread.__init__(self)
        # self.daemon = True
        self._port = port

    @property
    def roster(self):
        return _ROSTER

    @property
    def port(self):
        return self._port

    @staticmethod
    def set_callbacks():
        SetConnectCallback(pyconnect_callback)
        SetDisconnectCallback(pydisconnect_callback)
        SetReadCallback(pyread_callback)

    def stop(self):
        with nogil:
            StopServer();

    def run(self):
        logging.info("Starting Server on localhost:%i" % self.port)
        MessageServer.set_callbacks()
        cdef int cport = self.port
        with nogil:
            StartServer(cport)
        logging.info("Message Server Finished")
```

Then, as you would expect, we can start the thread by running this:

```python
# start libevent server
message_server = MessageServer(port)
message_server.start()
```

Notice that I specified `with nogil`. Our C code doesn't need the GIL since we are only using pure C types and not touching any Python runtime until the callbacks. Once the `libevent` socket server is running asynchronously, we can then move onto starting our flask web server:

```python
from flask import Flask
from flask import jsonify
```

```python
app = Flask("DashboardExample")
dashboard = None

@app.route("/")
def status():
    return jsonify(dashboard.roster.client_list())

class Dashboard:

    _port = None
    _roster = None

    def __init__(self, port, roster):
        global dashboard
        self._port = port
        self._roster = roster
        dashboard = self

    @property
    def port(self):
        return self._port

    @property
    def roster(self):
        return self._roster

    def start(self):
        app.run(port=self.port)
```

Flask is fantastic for writing RESTful Web Services. It's clean, simple, and most importantly, easy to use and read. This service returns the JSON representation of the client roster. Since I have encapsulated the roster object, I am using a simple global so that all the flask routes can query the correct context:

```python
# start webserver
dashboard = Dashboard(port, roster)
dashboard.start()
```

The web server now blocks until the kill signal is given. Then, it will return and we can then kill MessageServer:

```python
    # stop message server
message_server.stop()
```

Now, we listen onto the specified port in `server.cfg`:

```
[MessageServer]
port = 8080
webport = 8081
```

This roster object holds a list of clients and handles each callback:

```
class Roster:

    _clients = { }

    def handle_connect_event(self, client):
        """
        :returns True if client already exists else false
        """
        logging.info("connect: %s" % client)
        if client in self._clients:
            return True
        self._clients[client] = None
        return False;

    def handle_disconnect_event(self, client):
        logging.info("disconnect: %s" % client)
        self._clients.pop(client, None)

    def handle_read_event(self, client, message):
        logging.info("read: %s:[%s]" % (client, message))
        self._clients[client] = message

    def client_list(self):
        return self._clients
```

We run the server as follows:

```
$ python server --config=config.cfg
```

We can then connect clients using a simple telnet session:

```
$ telnet localhost 8080
```

We can type in messages, see it handled in the server log, and press *Q* to quit. We can then query the web service for the list of clients:

```
$ curl -X GET localhost:8081
{
  "127.0.0.1": "Hello World"
}
```

Caveat on GIL

There is a caveat to remember when using `gil`. In our callbacks, we need to acquire the GIL on each callback before we call any Python code; otherwise, we will segfault and get really confused. So, if you look into each of the `libevent` callbacks when calling the Cython functions, you have the following:

```
PyGILState_STATE gilstate_save = PyGILState_Ensure();
readcb (client, (char *)data);
PyGILState_Release(gilstate_save);
```

Notice that this is also called on the other two callbacks—firstly on the `discb` callback:

```
PyGILState_STATE gilstate_save = PyGILState_Ensure();
discb (client, NULL);
PyGILState_Release(gilstate_save);
```

Finally, on the connect callback, we must be a little safer and call it this way:

```
PyGILState_STATE gilstate_save = PyGILState_Ensure();
 if (!conncb (NULL, inet_ntoa (client_addr.sin_addr)))
   {
...
   }
 else
    close (client_fd);
 PyGILState_Release(gilstate_save);
```

We have to do this since we executed this with `nogil` from Cython. We need to acquire `gil` before we go back into the Python land. You really need to look at something like this with your creativity cap on and imagine what you could do with this. For example, you can use this as a way to capture data and use the Twisted Web server to implement an embedded RESTful server. Maybe, you can even use Python JSON to wrap data into nice objects. But, it demonstrates how you can really extend a fairly complicated piece of C software with something nice and of a high-level nature using Python libraries. This keeps everything very simple and maintainable instead of trying to do everything from scratch.

Unit testing the native code

Another use of Cython is unit testing the core functionality of shared C libraries. If you maintain a .pxd file (this is all you need really), you can write your own wrapper classes and do scalability testing of data structures with the expressiveness of Python. For example, we can write unit tests for something such as std::map and std::vector as follows:

```
from libcpp.vector cimport vector

PASSED = False

cdef vector[int] vect
cdef int i
for i in range(10):
    vect.push_back(i)
for i in range(10):
    print vect[i]

PASSED = True
```

Then, write a test for map as follows:

```
from libcpp.map cimport map

PASSED = False

cdef map[int,int] mymap
cdef int i
for i in range (10):
    mymap[i] = (i + 1)

for i in range (10):
    print mymap[i]

PASSED = True
```

Then, if we compile them into separate modules, we can simply write a test executor:

```
#!/usr/bin/env python
print "Cython C++ Unit test executor"

print "[TEST] std::map"
import testmap
assert testmap.PASSED
```

```
print "[PASS]"

print "[TEST] std::vec"
import testvec
assert testvec.PASSED
print "[PASS]"

print "Done..."
```

This is really trivial code, but it demonstrates the idea. If you put error handling with plenty of asserts and cause a fatal error, you can have some really nice unit testing against your C/C++ code. We can go further and implement this using Python's native unit testing framework.

Preventing subclassing

If you create an extension type in Cython, something you never want to be subclassed, it is a cpp class wrapped in a Python class. To prevent this, you can do the following:

```
cimport cython

@cython.final
cdef class A: pass

cdef class B (A): pass
```

This annotation will give an error when someone tries to subclass:

```
pycode.pyx:7:5: Base class 'A' of type 'B' is final
```

Note that these annotations only work on the cdef or cpdef functions and not on normal Python def functions.

Parsing large amounts of data

I want to try and prove how powerful and natively compiled C types are to programmers by showing the difference in parsing large amounts of XML. We can take the geographic data from the government as the test data for this experiment (http://www.epa.gov/enviro/geospatial-data-download-service).

Let's look at the size of this XML data:

```
ls -liah
total 480184
7849156 drwxr-xr-x    5 redbrain   staff    170B 25 Jul 16:42 ./
5803438 drwxr-xr-x   11 redbrain   staff    374B 25 Jul 16:41 ../
7849208 -rw-r--r--@   1 redbrain   staff    222M  9 Mar 04:27
EPAXMLDownload.xml
7849030 -rw-r--r--@   1 redbrain   staff     12M 25 Jul 16:38
EPAXMLDownload.zip
7849174 -rw-r--r--     1 redbrain   staff     57B 25 Jul 16:42 README
```

It's huge! Before we write programs, we need to understand a little bit about the structure of this data to see what we want to do with it. It contains facility site locations with addresses. This seems to be the bulk of the data in here, so let's try and parse it all out with a pure Python XML parser using the following:

```
from xml.etree import ElementTree as etree
```

The code uses etree to parse the XML file via the following:

```
xmlroot = etree.parse (__xmlFile)
```

Then, we look up the header and facilities via the following:

```
headers = xmlroot.findall ('Header')
facs = xmlroot.findall ('FacilitySite')
```

Finally, we output them into a file:

```
try:
    fd = open (__output, "wb")
    for i in facs:
        location = ""
        for y in i:
            if isinstance (y.text, basestring):
                location += y.tag + ": " + y.text + '\n'
        fd.write (location)
    # There is some dodgy unicode character
    # python doesn't like just ignore it
    except UnicodeEncodeError: pass
    except:
        print "Unexpected error:", sys.exc_info()[0]
        raise
    finally:
        if fd: fd.close ()
```

We then time the execution as follows:

```
10-4-5-52:bigData redbrain$ time python pyparse.py
USEPA Geospatial DataEnvironmental Protection AgencyUSEPA Geospatial
DataThis XML file was produced by US EPA and contains data specifying
the locations of EPA regulated facilities or cleanups that are being
provided by EPA for use by commercial mapping services and others
with an interest in using this information. Updates to this file
are produced on a regular basis by EPA and those updates as well as
documentation describing the contents of the file can be found at
URL:http://www.epa.gov/enviro
MAR-08-2013
[INFO] Number of Facilties 118421
[INFO] Dumping facilities to xmlout.dat

real    2m21.936s
user    1m58.260s
sys     0m9.5800s
```

This is quite long, but let's compare it using a different XML implementation — Python `lxml`. It's a different library implemented using Cython, but it implements the same library as the previous pure Python XML parser:

```
10-4-5-52:bigData redbrain$ sudo pip install lxml
```

We can simply drop the replacement import into the following:

```
from lxml import etree
```

The code stays the same, but the execution time is dramatically reduced (compile the Cython version by running `make` and the `cpyparse` binary is created from the same code with just a different import):

```
10-4-5-52:bigData redbrain$ time ./cpyparse
USEPA Geospatial DataEnvironmental Protection AgencyUSEPA Geospatial
DataThis XML file was produced by US EPA and contains data specifying
the locations of EPA regulated facilities or cleanups that are being
provided by EPA for use by commercial mapping services and others
with an interest in using this information. Updates to this file
are produced on a regular basis by EPA and those updates as well as
documentation describing the contents of the file can be found at
URL:http://www.epa.gov/enviro
MAR-08-2013
[INFO] Number of Facilties 118421
[INFO] Dumping facilities to xmlout.dat

real    0m7.874s
user    0m5.307s
sys     0m1.839s
```

You can really see the power of using native code when you make just a little effort. And to be finally assured that the code is the same, let's MD5 sum xmlout.dat that we created:

```
10-4-5-52:bigData redbrain$ md5 xmlout.dat xmlout.dat.cython
MD5 (xmlout.dat.python) = c2103a2252042f143489216b9c238283
MD5 (xmlout.dat.cython) = c2103a2252042f143489216b9c238283
```

So, you can see that the outputs are exactly the same just so we know that no funny business is going on. It's scary how much faster this can make your XML parsing; and if we calculate the speed increase rate, it is approximately 17.75 times faster; but don't take my word for it; try running it yourself. My MacBook has a solid state disk and has a 4 GB RAM with a 2 GHz Core 2 Duo.

Summary

Up to now, you will have seen the core of what's possible with Cython. In this chapter, we covered calling into C++ classes from Cython. You learned to wrap templates and even look at a more complex application demonstrating the usage of gil and nogil.

Chapter 6, Further Reading is the final chapter and will review some final caveats and usages with Cython. I will show how you can use Cython with Python 3. Finally, we will look at related projects and my opinions on their usages.

6
Further Reading

So far in this book, we have looked into both the basic and advanced topics of using Cython. But, it does not stop here; there are further topics that you can explore.

Overview

Other topics we will discuss in this chapter are OpenMP support, Cython's preprocessor and other related projects. Consider other implementations of Python such as PyPy or making it work with Python 3. Not only that but what are the Cython alter-natives and related Cython tools that are available. We will look at numba and Parakeet and look at numpy the flag ship usage of Cython.

OpenMP support

OpenMP is a standard API in the shared-memory parallel computing for languages; it's used in several open source projects such as ImageMagick (`http://www.imagemagick.org/`) to try and speed up the processing on large image manipulations. Cython has some support for this compiler extension. But, you must be aware that you need to use compilers such as GCC or MSVC, which support OpenMP. Clang/LLVM has no OpenMP support yet. This isn't really a place to explain when and why to use OpenMP since it is really a vast subject, but you should check out the following website: `http://docs.cython.org/src/userguide/parallelism.html`.

Compile time preprocessor

At compile time, similar to C/C++, we have the C-preprocessor to make some decisions on what gets compiled mostly from conditionals, defines, and a mixture of both. In Cython, we can replicate some of this behavior using IF, ELIF, ELSE, and DEF. This is demonstrated as an example in the following code line:

```
DEF myConstant = "hello cython"
```

We also have access to os.uname as predefined constants from the Cython compiler:

- UNAME_SYSNAME
- UNAME_NODENAME
- UNAME_RELEASE
- UNAME_VERSION
- UNAME_MACHINE

We can also run conditional expressions against these as follows:

```
IF UNAME_SYSNAME == "Windows":
    include "windows.pyx"
ELSE:
    include "unix.pyx"
```

You also have ELIF to use in conditional expressions. If you compare something as this against some of your headers in C programs, you will see how you can replicate basic C-preprocessor behavior in Cython. This gives you a quick idea of how you can replicate C-preprocessor usage in your headers.

Python 3

Porting to Python 3 can be painful, but reading around the subject shows us that people have had success porting their code to 3.*x* by simply compiling their module with Cython instead of actually porting their code! With Cython, you can specify the output to conform to the Python 3 API via the following:

```
$ cython -3 <options>
```

This will make sure you are outputting Python 3 stuff instead of the default argument of -2, which generates for the 2.*x* standard.

PyPy

PyPy has become a popular alternative to the standard Python implementation. More importantly, it is now being used by many companies (small and large) in their production environments to boost performance and scalability. How does PyPy differ from normal CPython? While the latter is a traditional interpreter, the former is a full-fledged virtual machine. It maintains a just-in-time compiler backend for runtime optimization on most relevant architectures.

Getting Cythonized modules to run on PyPy is dependent on their **cpyext** emulation layer. This isn't quite complete and has many inconsistencies. But, if you are brave and up to trying it out, it's going to get better and better with each release.

AutoPXD

When it comes to writing Cython modules most of your work will comprise of getting your pxd declarations correct so that you can manipulate native code correctly. There are several projects attempting to create a compiler to read C/C++ headers and generate your pxd declarations as output. The main issue is maintaining a fully compliant C and C++ parser. Part of my Google Summer of Code project was to use the Python plugin system as part of GCC to reuse GCC's code for parsing C/C++ code. The plugin could intercept the declarations, types and prototypes. It isn't fully ready for use and there are other similar projects attempting the same issue. More information can be found at `https://github.com/cython/cython/wiki/AutoPxd`.

Pyrex and Cython

Cython is a derivative of Pyrex.. However Pyrex is more primitive, Cython provides us with much more powerful typing and features as well as optimizations and confidence with exception handling.

SWIG and Cython

Overall, if you consider SWIG (`http://swig.org/`) as a way to write a native Python module, you could be fooled to think that Cython and SWIG are similar. SWIG is mainly used to write wrappers for language bindings. For example, if you have some C code as follows:

```
int myFunction (int, const char *){ … }
```

You can write the SWIG interface file as follows:

```
/* example.i */
%module example
%{
  extern int myFunction (int, const char *);
...
%}
```

Compile this with the following:

```
$ swig -python example.i
```

You can compile and link the module as you would do for a Cython output since this generates the necessary C code. This is fine if you want a basic module to simply call into C from Python. But Cython provides users with much more.

Cython is much more developed and optimized, and it truly understands how to work with C types and memory management and how to handle exceptions. With SWIG, you cannot manipulate data; you simply call into functions on the C side from Python. In Cython, we can call C from Python and vice versa. The type conversion is just so powerful; not only this, we can also wrap C types into real Python classes to make C data feel Pythonic.

The XML example from *Chapter 5, Advanced Cython*, where we were able to drop in the import replacement? This is possible because of Cython's type conversion, and the API is very Pythonic. Not only can we wrap C types into Pythonic objects, but we also let Cython generate the boilerplate necessary for Python to do this without wrapping things into a class. What's more is that Cython produces a much more optimized code for the user.

Cython and NumPy

NumPy is a scientific library designed to provide functionality similar to or on par with MATLAB, which is a paid proprietary mathematics package. NumPy has a lot of popularity with Cython users since you can seek out more performance from your highly computational code using C types. In Cython, you can import this library as follows:

```
import numpy as np
cimport numpy as np

np.import_array()
```

You can access full Python APIs as follows:

```
np.PyArray_ITER_NOTDONE
```

So, you can integrate with iterators at a very native area of the API. This allows NumPy users to get a lot of speed when working with native types via something as follows:

```
cdef double * val = (<double*>np.PyArray_MultiIter_DATA(it, 0))[0]
```

We can cast the data from the array to `double`, and it's a `cdef` type in Cython to work with now. For more information and NumPy tutorials, visit `https://github.com/cython/cython/wiki/tutorials-numpy`.

Numba versus Cython

Numba is another way to get your Python code to become almost native to your host system by outputting the code to be run on LLVM seamlessly. Numba makes use of decorators such as the following:

```
@autojit
def myFunction (): ...
```

Numba also integrates with NumPy. On the whole, it sounds great. Unlike Cython, you only apply decorators to pure Python code, and it does everything for you, but you may find that the optimizations will be fewer and not as powerful.

Numba does not integrate with C/C++ to the extent that Cython does. If you want it to integrate, you need to use **Foreign Function Interfaces (FFI)** to wrap calls. You also need to define structs and work with C types in Python code in a very abstract sense to a point where you don't really have much control as compared with Cython.

Numba is mostly comprised of decorators, such as `@locals`, from Cython. But in the end, all this creates is just-in-time-compiled functions with a proper native function signature. Since you can specify the typing of function calls, this should provide more native speed when calling and returning data from functions. I would argue that the optimizations you will get as compared to Cython will be minimal as you might need a lot of abstractions to talk to the native code; although, calling in a lot of functions might be a faster technique.

Just for reference, LLVM is a low-level virtual machine; it's a compiler development infrastructure where projects can use it as a JIT compiler. The infrastructure can be extended to run things, such as pure Java byte-code and even Python via Numba. It can be used for almost any purpose with a nice API for development. As opposed to GCC (an ahead-of-time compiler infrastructure), which implements a lot of static analysis ahead of time before code is run, LLVM allows code to change at runtime.

 For more information on Numba and LLVM, you can refer to either of the following links:

http://numba.pydata.org/

http://llvm.org/

Parakeet and Numba

Parakeet is another project that works alongside Numba, adding extremely specific optimizations to the Python code that uses lots of nested loops and parallelism. As with OpenMP, where it's really cool, Numba too requires using annotations on your code to do all this for the programmer. The downside is that you won't just magically optimize any Python code, the optimization that Parakeet does is on very specific sets of code.

Relevant Links

Some useful links for referencing are:

- https://github.com/cython/cython/wiki/FAQ
- https://github.com/cython/cython/wiki
- http://cython.org/
- http://www.cosc.canterbury.ac.nz/greg.ewing/python/Pyrex/
- http://swig.org/
- http://www.numpy.org/
- http://wiki.cython.org/tutorials/numpy
- http://en.wikipedia.org/wiki/NumPy
- http://llvm.org/
- http://numba.pydata.org/
- http://numba.pydata.org/numba-doc/0.9/interface_c.html
- http://gcc.gnu.org/

Summary

If you've read this far, you should now be familiar with Cython to such an extent that you can embed it with C bindings and even make some of your pure Python code more efficient. I've shown you how to apply Cython against an actual open source project and even how to extend native software with a Twisted Web server! As I kept saying throughout the book, it makes C feel as though there are endless possibilities to control logic or that you can extend the system with the plethora of Python modules available. Thanks for reading.

Index

Symbols

E

emacs mode 2
enums 14
exceptions 60, 61

F

Foreign Function Interfaces (FFI) 81
function pointers 15

G

garbage collector, Python 32-34
GDB
  about 47
  using, with Cython 47
GIL
  about 66
  caveat 71
gil keyword 67
Global Interpreter Lock. *See* GIL
GNU/Autotools 27, 28
GNU Project Debugger. *See* GDB

H

Hello World program 3, 4

I

ImageMagick
  reference link 77
includes 4
installing
  Cython 2

L

linking models 10, 11
LLVM
  reference link 82
logging from C/C++, into Python 18-21

M

Makefiles
  avoiding 32
mathematical application,
      Cython documentation 30
messaging server 67-70
mutex 66

N

namespaces
  about 58
  caveat 65
native code
  unit testing 72, 73
new keyword 59
nogil keyword 67
Numba
  about 82
  reference link 82
  versus Cython 81
NumPy
  about 80
  reference link 81

O

OpenMP 77
overloading 62-64

P

Parakeet 82
parallelism
  reference link 77
public keyword 16, 17
PyPy
  using 79
Pyrex
  versus Cython 79
Python
  C functions, calling from 5, 6
  embedding 38, 39
  garbage collector 32-34

Thank you for buying
Learning Cython Programming
Second Edition

About Packt Publishing

Packt, pronounced 'packed', published its first book, *Mastering phpMyAdmin for Effective MySQL Management*, in April 2004, and subsequently continued to specialize in publishing highly focused books on specific technologies and solutions.

Our books and publications share the experiences of your fellow IT professionals in adapting and customizing today's systems, applications, and frameworks. Our solution-based books give you the knowledge and power to customize the software and technologies you're using to get the job done. Packt books are more specific and less general than the IT books you have seen in the past. Our unique business model allows us to bring you more focused information, giving you more of what you need to know, and less of what you don't.

Packt is a modern yet unique publishing company that focuses on producing quality, cutting-edge books for communities of developers, administrators, and newbies alike. For more information, please visit our website at www.packtpub.com.

About Packt Open Source

In 2010, Packt launched two new brands, Packt Open Source and Packt Enterprise, in order to continue its focus on specialization. This book is part of the Packt Open Source brand, home to books published on software built around open source licenses, and offering information to anybody from advanced developers to budding web designers. The Open Source brand also runs Packt's Open Source Royalty Scheme, by which Packt gives a royalty to each open source project about whose software a book is sold.

Writing for Packt

We welcome all inquiries from people who are interested in authoring. Book proposals should be sent to author@packtpub.com. If your book idea is still at an early stage and you would like to discuss it first before writing a formal book proposal, then please contact us; one of our commissioning editors will get in touch with you.

We're not just looking for published authors; if you have strong technical skills but no writing experience, our experienced editors can help you develop a writing career, or simply get some additional reward for your expertise.

[PACKT] open source
PUBLISHING
community experience distilled

Python Network Programming Cookbook

Over 70 detailed recipes to develop practical solutions for a wide range of real-world network programming tasks

Dr. M. O. Faruque Sarker

Python Network Programming Cookbook

ISBN: 978-1-84951-346-3   Paperback: 234 pages

Over 70 detailed recipes to develop practical solutions for a wide range of real-world network programming tasks

1. Demonstrates how to write various besopke client/server networking applications using standard and popular third-party Python libraries.

2. Learn how to develop client programs for networking protocols such as HTTP/HTTPS, SMTP, POP3, FTP, CGI, XML-RPC, SOAP and REST.

Learning IPython for Interactive Computing and Data Visualization

Learn IPython for interactive Python programming, high-performance numerical computing, and data visualization

Cyrille Rossant

Learning IPython for Interactive Computing and Data Visualization

ISBN: 978-1-78216-993-2   Paperback: 138 pages

Learn IPython for interactive Python programming, high-performance numerical computing, and data visualization

1. A practical step-by-step tutorial which will help you to replace the Python console with the powerful IPython command-line interface.

2. Use the IPython notebook to modernize the way you interact with Python.

3. Perform highly efficient computations with NumPy and Pandas.

Please check **www.PacktPub.com** for information on our titles

Learning Geospatial Analysis with Python

ISBN: 978-1-78328-113-8   Paperback: 364 pages

Master GIS and Remote Sensing analysis using Python with these easy to follow tutorials

1. Construct applications for GIS development by exploiting Python.

2. Focuses on built-in Python modules and libraries compatible with the Python Packaging Index distribution system – no compiling of C libraries necessary.

3. This is a practical, hands-on tutorial that teaches you all about Geospatial analysis in Python.

Python Testing Cookbook

ISBN: 978-1-84951-466-8   Paperback: 364 pages

Over 70 simple but incredibly effective recipes for taking control of automated testing using powerful Python testing tools

1. Learn to write tests at every level using a variety of Python testing tools.

2. The first book to include detailed screenshots and recipes for using Jenkins continuous integration server (formerly known as Hudson).

3. Explore innovative ways to introduce automated testing to legacy systems.

4. Written by Greg L. Turnquist – senior software engineer and author of Spring Python 1.1.

Please check **www.PacktPub.com** for information on our titles

Made in the USA
San Bernardino, CA
16 April 2016